Hiking Carlsbad Caverns and Guadalupe Mountains National Parks

Help Us Keep This Guide Up to Date

Every effort has been made by the author and editors to make this guide as accurate and useful as possible. However, many things can change after a guide is published—trails are rerouted, regulations change, techniques evolve, facilities come under new management, etc.

We would love to hear from you concerning your experiences with this guide and how you feel it could be improved and kept up to date. While we may not be able to respond to all comments and suggestions, we'll take them to heart, and we'll also make certain to share them with the author. Please send your comments and suggestions to the following address:

The Globe Pequot Press
Reader Response/Editorial Department
P.O. Box 480
Guilford, CT 06437

Or you may e-mail us at:

editorial@GlobePequot.com

Thanks for your input, and happy trails!

Hiking Carlsbad Caverns and Guadalupe Mountains National Parks

Second Edition

Bill Schneider

Published in partnership with the
Carlsbad Caverns–Guadalupe Mountains Association

FALCON®

GUILFORD, CONNECTICUT
HELENA, MONTANA

AN IMPRINT OF THE GLOBE PEQUOT PRESS

A FALCON GUIDE

"It seems that the strangeness and wonder are emphasized here in the desert. . . .
The extreme clarity of the desert light is equaled by the extreme
individualism of desert life forms."
—Edward Abbey

Contents

Foreword ix

Acknowledgments x

Introduction 1

    How to Use This Guide 3

    Zero Impact 9

    Be Prepared 11

    Desert Hiking 13

    Hiker's Checklist 16

Carlsbad Caverns National Park 21

Surface Routes 23

    1. Chihuahuan Desert Nature Trail 23

    2. Guano Road Trail 26

    3. Juniper Ridge 29

    4. Rattlesnake Canyon 31

    5. Guadalupe Ridge 35

    6. Slaughter Canyon 38

    7. Yucca Canyon 41

Cave Routes 46

    8. Natural Entrance 49

    9. The Big Room 51

    10. King's Palace 52

    11. Lefthand Tunnel 53

    12. Slaughter Canyon Cave 54

    13. Lower Cave 56

    14. Spider Cave 57

    15. Hall of the White Giant 58

Guadalupe Mountains National Park 61

Pine Springs Trailhead 64

    16. The Pinery 65

    17. Salt Basin Overlook 67

    18. El Capitan 69

    19. Guadalupe Peak 73

    20. Devil's Hall 77

    21. Hunter Peak 80

    22. The Bowl 85

    23. Smith Spring 89

    24. Foothills 92

    25. Bush Mountain 94

    26. Pine Springs to McKittrick Canyon 99

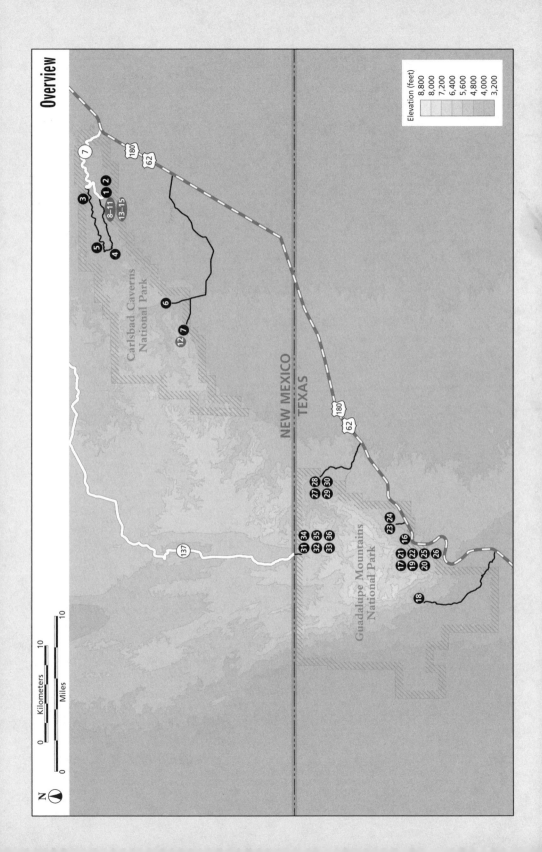

Overview

McKittrick Canyon Trailhead 104
   27. McKittrick Canyon Nature Trail 106
   28. McKittrick Canyon 108
   29. McKittrick Ridge 112
   30. Permian Reef 116

Dog Canyon Trailhead 119
   31. Indian Meadow Nature Trail 120
   32. Lost Peak 122
   33. Blue Ridge 124
   34. Marcus Trail 128
   35. Tejas Trail 132
   36. Dog Canyon to McKittrick Canyon 136

Afterword: The Value of Guidebooks 140
Vacation Planner 142
Author's Recommendations 144
About the Author 147

Foreword

I was only fourteen years old at the time when I first set sight on the Guadalupe Mountains. I was relocating from a large metropolitan area in Japan, and after our plane landed in El Paso, my family and I started on our journey eastward toward Carlsbad, New Mexico. That's when I saw what appeared to be a gigantic piece of rock protruding from the earth. This encounter was my first face-to-face meeting with the Guadalupe Mountains. Back then I had no idea that the summit at Guadalupe Peak is the highest point in Texas (8,749 feet) or that beneath the barren desert there are miles of secret chambers filled with astonishing cave formations.

Our organization, Carlsbad Caverns–Guadalupe Mountains Association (CCGMA), was commissioned in 1957 to support the purposes and mission of the National Park Service. Our goals are met by providing interpretive materials to our park visitors, especially to visitors like myself back when I first came to this area. This guidebook describes what types of tours are available at both parks. It also provides details about the gear you will need, hiking safety, and the highlights of each tour.

The most notable feature of this guidebook is the multilateral cooperation involved in publishing it. FalconGuides, the National Park Service, and the CCGMA have put in a tremendous amount of time, effort, and resources in completing this book. It is our hope that every reader of this guidebook will become well informed on all aspects of each hike and tour so that he or she can enjoy, cherish, and protect our American heritage.

As for me, even thirty-five years later I am still amazed each time I visit both Carlsbad Caverns and Guadalupe Mountains National Parks. The magnificent Temple of the Sun in the Big Room, McKittrick's fall color, the enchanting "twilight zone" at the Natural Entrance, or just the simple cactus blooms in spring reminds me of how great the wonders of the Southwest desert really are.

Read on, and let's experience America's treasures.

T. K. Kajiki
Executive Director
Carlsbad Caverns–Guadalupe Mountains Association

Acknowledgments

Any book—and especially a trail guide—is a cooperative effort, and this book is an excellent example of how cooperation can result in a superior product. To put it mildly, I received help from many people.

Rick LoBello, former executive of the Carlsbad Caverns–Guadalupe Mountains Association, was a spearhead in getting the original book published back in 1996. His associate at the time, Patsy Solwell, also helped in several ways.

Many National Park Service staffers also helped me research and review the original book. In no particular order, they are Rich McCamant, Gary Veguist, Ed Greene, Dale Pate, Doug Ballou, Cookie Ballou, Rick Jackson, Dan Cantu, Vivian Sartori, Sam Franco, Dave Roemer, Rick Moraine, Karen Carswell, and Linda Burlingame.

In this revised second edition of the book, I once again worked closely with many people in reviewing and updating the material. T. K. Kajiki, current executive director of the CCGMA, helped coordinate the review, as did these NPS staffers (again in no particular order)—Carolyn Richard, Dale Pate, Paula Bauer, Doug Buehler, and Tony Armijo.

Special thanks to all who helped make this book a reality.

Introduction

Driving along the "National Park Highway" (U.S. Highway 62/180) through Guadalupe Pass between the Delaware and Guadalupe Mountains, through the eastern flank of Guadalupe Mountains National Park, and by the front door of Carlsbad Caverns National Park, you might glance off to the western horizon and see some hills but not realize that you have seen the Great Reef.

This is the home of two national parks, and it is one of the most cave-rich areas on the planet. It has so many caves that a cross section would look like a 20-mile-long chunk of Swiss cheese.

It certainly looks like a mountain range, but technically, geologists call these 8,000-foot peaks the Capitan Reef. Geologists come from all over the world to see this giant, exposed formation composed of ancient fossils and riddled with caves.

An aerial view of the Guadalupe Mountains and the mouth of the McKittrick Canyon. NPS PHOTO.

Lechuguilla, common in both parks. NPS PHOTO BY D. ALLEN.

The reef rises slowly in southeastern New Mexico, site of Carlsbad Caverns National Park, and extends southward into northwestern Texas, where it abruptly ends with the venerable El Capitan at the southern edge of Guadalupe Mountains National Park. It seems the entire reef should be one national park, but 10 miles of the Lincoln National Forest separate the two parks.

The area doesn't have a Grand Teton or Denali, but so what? It has a special beauty that those famous mountains could never match. That beauty is embodied in the rugged individualism of desert flora and fauna and in the incredible diversity found in the parks, with the caves adding an extra treat to the mix.

When you go to Yellowstone, you study geysers. When you go to Point Reyes, you learn about elephant seals. When you go to Olympic, you learn about rain forests. When you go to Hawaii Volcanoes, you learn about volcanoes. When you go to Carlsbad Caverns, you learn about caves. And when you go to Guadalupe Mountains, you learn about the incredible diversity of desert flora and fauna found in this corner of the Chihuahuan Desert.

If that's not reason enough to come to Carlsbad Caverns or Guadalupe Mountains National Parks, here's another small bonus: Neither park has entrance fees for surface use. However, there are camping fees for the drive-in campgrounds, and in some cases you pay a small fee for entering sections of Carlsbad Caverns and other caves.

How to Use This Guide

This guidebook won't answer every question you have about your planned excursions to Carlsbad Caverns and Guadalupe Mountains National Parks. But then, you probably do not want to know everything before you go, lest you eliminate the thrill of making your own discoveries. This book does, however, provide much of the basic information you need to plan your hiking trip.

Types of Trips

Loop: Starts and finishes at the same trailhead, with no (or very little) retracing of your steps.

Shuttle: A point-to-point trip that requires two vehicles or an arrangement to be picked up at the end of the trail at a designated time. One way to manage the logistical problems of shuttles is to arrange for another party to start at the other end of the trail, meet at a predetermined point on the trail and trade keys, and, when finished hiking, drive each other's vehicle home.

Out and back: Traveling to a specific destination and then retracing your steps back to the trailhead.

Distances

In Guadalupe Mountains National Park, distances used in this book come from National Park Service (NPS) handouts and National Geographic Trails Illustrated maps. In Carlsbad Caverns National Park, distances come from NPS handouts and signs and, in a few cases, estimates made from topo maps. Keep in mind that distance is often less important than difficulty. A rocky, 2-mile uphill climb can take longer than 4 miles on a well-contoured trail on flat terrain.

Ratings

The estimates of difficulty should serve as general guidelines only, not the final word. What is difficult to one person may be easy to the next. In this guidebook difficulty ratings consider both how long and how strenuous the route is. Here are general definitions of the ratings.

Easy: Suitable for any hiker, including small children or the elderly, without serious elevation gain, hazardous sections, or places where the trail is faint.

Moderate: Suitable for hikers who have some experience and at least an average fitness level, probably not suitable for small children or the elderly unless they have above-average level of fitness, perhaps with some short sections where the trail is difficult to follow, and often with some hills to climb.

Cairns lead the way through the junipers dotting the plateau above Yucca Canyon.

Difficult: Suitable for experienced hikers with above-average fitness level, often with sections of the trail that are difficult to follow or some off-trail sections that could require knowledge of route-finding with topo map and compass, sometimes with serious elevation gain, and possibly some hazardous conditions.

Maps

The maps in this book serve as a general guide only. You should obtain more detailed maps to take with you or your hikes. Good maps are easy to find, and they are essential to any wilderness trip. For safety reasons, you need maps for route-finding and for "staying found." For non-safety reasons, you would not want to miss out on the unending joy of mindlessly whittling away untold hours staring at a topo map and wondering what it's like here and there.

For trips into the Carlsbad Caverns and Guadalupe Mountains National Parks, you have two good choices for maps—U.S. Geological Survey (USGS) topo maps and National Geographic Trails Illustrated maps. The well-prepared wilderness traveler will take both. Guadalupe Mountains National Park also has a free map that is adequate for many hikes.

You can find maps at the following locations:

National Geographic Trails Illustrated maps: You can buy these maps in bookstores managed by the Carlsbad Caverns–Guadalupe Mountains Association in both parks or order them online at www.ccgma.org. You can also order them by calling (800) 962–1643.

USGS: These maps are available at sporting goods stores in the local area, or write directly to the USGS at the following address: Map Distribution, U.S. Geological Survey, Box 25286, Federal Center, Denver, CO 80225.

For More Information

The best source of additional information is the National Park Service. Use the following addresses and phone numbers.

Carlsbad Caverns National Park
3225 National Park Highway
Carlsbad, NM 88220
Phone: (505) 785–2232
www.nps.gov/cave

Guadalupe Mountains National Park
H.C. 60, Box 400
Salt Flat, TX 79847-9400
Phone: (915) 828–3251
www.nps.gov/gamo

Following Faint Trails

Some trails in both parks receive infrequent use and can fade away in places. Don't panic. Usually these sections are short and you can look ahead to see where the trail goes. If so, focus on that landmark and don't worry about being off the trail for a short distance.

You should also watch for other indicators that you are indeed on the right route even if the trail isn't clearly visible. In Carlsbad Caverns and Guadalupe Mountains, watch for cairns (strategically located piles of rocks), which are often used to mark faint trails. Please don't build new cairns; this can make a confusing situation worse.

Sharing

We all want our own wilderness area all to ourselves, but that only happens in our dreams. Lots of people use the national parks, and to give everybody an equal chance of having a great experience, we all must work at politely sharing the wilderness.

For example, hikers must share trails with backcountry horse riders. Both groups have every right to be on the trail. Keep in mind that horses and other stock animals are much less maneuverable than hikers, so it becomes the hiker's responsibility to yield the right-of-way. When you see horses ahead on the trail or when they catch you from behind, move uphill from the trail about 20 feet and quietly let the stock animals pass.

Another example of politely sharing the wilderness is courteously choosing your campsite. If you get to a popular camping area late in the day and all the good campsites are taken, don't crowd in on another camper. This is most aggravating, as these

The 1989 El Capitan fire was caused by a lightning strike. Other fires in the parks have been caused by careless park visitors, so be careful with fire. NPS PHOTO BY J. BASSINGER.

sites rightfully go on a first-come, first-served basis. If you're late, you have the responsibility to move on or take a campsite a respectable distance away from other campers, even if it's a less desirable site. In Guadalupe Mountains National Park, designated backcountry campgrounds have as many as eight tent sites. Try to pick one as far away from other campers as possible.

Special Rules and Regulations for Backcountry Use

Carlsbad Caverns and Guadalupe Mountains National Parks have strict regulations to protect the fragile environment. Please follow these rules carefully.

- Pets, with or without a leash, are prohibited on all backcountry trails.
- Do not drive vehicles off established roads.
- The collecting, destroying, or defacing of any mineral, plant, animal, or historic or archaeological artifact is prohibited.
- All firearms, or any implement designed to discharge missiles, are prohibited.
- Entry into any cave in the backcountry without written permission from the park superintendent is prohibited.

- Campfires are prohibited.
- All backcountry campers must have a free backcountry camping permit. In Guadalupe Mountains, backpackers must use designated campsites. In Carlsbad Caverns, campsites must be located (a) at least 100 feet off established trails, (b) 0.25 mile from any water source, (c) 100 yards from any cave entrance, and (d) 0.5 mile from any road or designated day use area.
- Camping is allowed only in designated Wilderness.
- Backcountry camping groups are limited to ten people. Larger groups must hike and camp at least 0.25 mile apart in separate areas.
- You must carry your backcountry permit with you at all times.
- Vehicle or RV camping is prohibited.
- Your safety is your responsibility. Be prepared for trail and weather conditions. Hike carefully. Be sure that someone, a friend or family member, knows when to expect your return and will contact the park office if you are overdue.

Horses

Horses are allowed on backcountry trails in both Carlsbad Caverns and Guadalupe Mountains under special regulations. About 60 percent of the trails in Guadalupe Mountains and most of the trails in Carlsbad Caverns are open to horses, but an essential part of planning a trip involving horses or other stock animals should be a call to the park headquarters for specific regulations.

Some trails are simply too hazardous, and these have been closed to horse use. In other areas trails pass through a particularly fragile environment intolerant to horse use. For example, horse manure may introduce exotic plant species that can displace native vegetation.

Guadalupe Mountains has prepared a special "Horseback Riding" brochure explaining in detail the park regulations. It also includes an excellent trail map showing which trails are open to horses and ranking the trails for difficulty.

Although you should definitely call for specific information, here is a brief checklist of special needs and regulations for horse use in Carlsbad Caverns and Guadalupe Mountains National Parks.

- All rides in the parks require thorough preparation. Improper equipment, poor conditioning, or disregard for weather conditions can result in an unpleasant or dangerous experience.
- Both parks require a free backcountry use permit for all horse use of backcountry trails. You can get the permits at any park visitor center or ranger station.
- Horse use is restricted to day use only. No horses can be kept in the backcountry overnight.
- Both parks have stock corrals, but you must call ahead for reservations. Manure dropped in the corrals must be cleaned up and deposited in a marked receptacle

before you leave the park. Trail riders must use the trailheads at these corrals instead of transporting horses to other trailheads.

- No feed is available in either park.
- Water is available at corrals, but no water is available along backcountry trails in either park.
- All stock should be properly shod before arriving at the park. Bring shoeing tools and supplies. Almost all trails have rocky sections.
- Groups are limited to ten animals or fewer. This is to reduce potential conflicts between trail riders and hikers and to reduce trail damage.
- All stock must remain on designated trails.
- All livestock must meet state vaccination requirements, and copies of vaccination documents must be in your possession. Nursing colts may not accompany their mothers on park trails, and loose herding is not permitted.
- Special use permits are required for commercial groups.
- No horses are available for rent in the vicinity of either park.

Zero Impact

Going into the desert is like visiting a famous museum. You obviously do not want to leave your mark on an art treasure in the museum. If everybody going through the museum left one little mark, the piece of art would be quickly destroyed. And of what value is a big building full of trashed art? The same goes for a pristine wilderness, such as the Chihuahuan Desert of Carlsbad Caverns and Guadalupe Mountains National Parks, which is as magnificent as any masterpiece of any artist. If we all left just one little mark, the wilderness would soon be despoiled.

A wilderness can accommodate lots of human use as long as everybody behaves. But a few thoughtless or uninformed visitors can ruin it for the rest of us. An important addition to the hiker's checklist is proper wilderness manners. Don't leave home without them.

All wilderness users have a responsibility to know and follow the rules of zero-impact camping. An important source of these guidelines is the book, *Wild Country Companion* (Globe Pequot, 1994).

Nowadays, most wilderness users want to walk softly, but some aren't aware that they have poor manners. Often, their actions are dictated by the outdated understanding of a past generation of campers who cut green boughs for evening shelters, built campfires with fire rings, and dug trenches around tents. In the 1950s, these "camping rules" may have been acceptable, but they leave long-lasting scars. Today,

◀ *The New Mexico century plant only blooms once, usually after twenty or thirty years, not one hundred years as rumored.* NPS PHOTO BY D. ALLEN.

In backcountry campsites in the Guadalupe Mountains, the NPS has designated specific flattened out tent sites such as this one at the Blue Ridge Camp.

such behavior is absolutely unacceptable. The wilderness is shrinking, and the number of users is mushrooming. More and more camping areas show the unsightly signs of this trend.

Thus, a new code of ethics is growing out of necessity to cope with the unending waves of people wanting a perfect wilderness experience. Today, we all must leave no signs that we have gone before. Canoeists can look behind them and see no trace of their passing. Hikers should have the same goal. Enjoy the wildness, but zero impact, of your visit.

Most of us know better than to litter—in or out of the wilderness. Be sure you leave nothing, regardless of how small it is, along the trail or at the campsite. This means you should pack out everything, including orange peels, flip tops, cigarette butts, and gum wrappers. Also, pick up any trash that others leave behind.

Follow the main trail. Avoid cutting switchbacks and walking on vegetation beside the trail. In the desert, some of the terrain is very fragile, so stay on the trail. And don't pick up "souvenirs," such as rocks, antlers, or wildflowers. The next person wants to see them, too. Besides, this violates park regulations.

This goes triple for any archaeological sites. They are very precious and extra fragile. Don't even go near them, and obviously, do not disturb the aging signs of early cultures. Park regulations strictly prohibit disturbing archaeological sites.

Avoid making loud noises that may disturb others. Remember, sound travels easily to the other side of the canyon. Be courteous.

Be careful with food wastes to prevent unsightly messes and bad odors.

If you use toilet paper, you need to pack it out with the rest of your garbage. In many hiking areas, you can safely use white, unscented paper and bury it along with human waste about 6–8 inches deep, but at Carlsbad Caverns and Guadalupe Mountains, the topsoil is so thin that you really only have one option—packing it out. Bring along ziplock bags for this purpose.

Finally, and perhaps most important, strictly follow the pack-in pack-out rule. If you carry something into the backcountry, consume it or carry it out.

Leave zero impact—and then, put your ear to the ground in the wilderness and listen carefully. Thousands of people who will follow you are thanking you for your courtesy and good sense.

Be Prepared

The Scouts have been guided for decades by, perhaps, the best single piece of safety advice—Be Prepared! For starters, this means carrying survival and first-aid materials, proper clothing, compass, and topographic map—and knowing how to use them.

Perhaps the second-best advice is to tell somebody where you're going and when you plan to return. Pilots must file flight plans before every trip, and anybody venturing into a blank spot on the map should do the same. File your "flight plan" with a friend or relative before taking off.

Close behind filing a flight plan and being prepared with proper equipment is the importance of physical conditioning. Being fit not only makes wilderness travel more fun, it makes it safer.

To whet your appetite for more knowledge of wilderness safety and preparedness, here are a few basic tips.

- Check the weather forecast. Be careful not to get caught at high altitude by a bad storm, and watch the cloud formations closely so that you don't get stranded on a ridgeline during a lightning storm. Avoid traveling during prolonged periods of cold weather.
- Avoid traveling alone in the wilderness.
- Keep your party together.
- Know the preventive measures, symptoms, and treatment of hypothermia, the silent killer.
- Study basic survival and first-aid before leaving home.
- Don't eat wild plants unless you are positive of their identification.

- Before you leave find out as much as you can about the route, especially the potential hazards.
- Don't exhaust yourself or other members of your party by traveling too far or too fast. Let the slowest person set the pace.
- Don't wait until you're confused to look at your maps. Follow them as you go along, from the moment you start moving up the trail, so you have a continual fix on your location.
- If you get lost, don't panic. Sit down and relax for a few minutes while you carefully check your topo map and take a reading with your compass. Confidently plan your next move. It's often smart to retrace your steps until you find familiar ground, even if you think it might make the trip longer. Lots of people get temporarily lost in the wilderness and survive—usually by calmly and rationally dealing with the situation.
- Stay clear of all wild animals.

Last but not least, don't forget that the best defense against unexpected hazards is knowledge. Read the wilderness safety information presented in *Wild Country Companion* (Globe Pequot, 1994).

Lightning
Do not be caught on a ridge or a mountaintop, under large solitary trees, in the open, or near open water during a lightning storm. Try to seek shelter in a low-lying area, ideally in a dense stand of small, uniformly sized trees. Stay away from anything that might attract lightning, such as metal tent poles, graphite fishing rods, or pack frames.

Survival Kit
A survival kit should include: compass, whistle, matches in a waterproof container, cigarette lighter, candle, signal mirror, fire starter, aluminum foil, water purification tablets, space blanket, and flare.

First-Aid Kit
Your first-aid kit should include: a sewing needle, a snakebite kit, aspirin, codeine tablets, antibacterial ointment, two antiseptic swabs, two butterfly bandages, adhesive tape, four adhesive strips, four gauze pads, two triangular bandages, moleskin, one roll of 3-inch gauze, CPR shield, rubber gloves, and lightweight first-aid instructions.

The Silent Killer
Be aware of the danger of hypothermia—a condition in which the body's internal temperature drops below normal. It can lead to mental and physical collapse and death.

Hypothermia is caused by exposure to cold and is aggravated by wetness, wind, and exhaustion. The moment you begin to lose heat faster than your body produces it, you're suffering from exposure. Your body starts involuntary exercise such as shivering to stay warm, and your body makes involuntary adjustments to preserve normal temperature in vital organs, restricting blood flow to the extremities.

Both responses drain your energy reserves. The only way to stop the drain is to reduce the degree of exposure.

With full-blown hypothermia, your energy reserves are exhausted and cold reaches the brain, depriving you of good judgment and reasoning power. You won't be aware that this is happening. You lose control of your hands. Your internal temperature slides downward. Without treatment, this slide leads to stupor, collapse, and death.

To defend against hypothermia, stay dry. When clothes get wet, they lose about 90 percent of their insulating value. Wool loses relatively less heat; cotton, down, and some synthetics lose more. Choose rain clothes that cover the head, neck, body, and legs, and provide good protection against wind-driven rain. Most cases of hypothermia develop in air temperatures between thirty and fifty degrees Fahrenheit, but they can also develop in warmer temperatures.

If your party is exposed to wind, cold, and wet, think hypothermia. Watch yourself and others for these symptoms: uncontrollable fits of shivering; vague, slow, slurred speech; memory lapses; incoherence; immobile, fumbling hands; frequent stumbling or a lurching gait; drowsiness (to sleep is to die); apparent exhaustion; and inability to get up after a rest.

When a member of your party has hypothermia, he/she may deny any problem. Believe the symptoms, not the victim. Even mild symptoms demand treatment, as follows:

- Get the victim out of the wind and rain.
- Strip off all wet clothes.
- If the victim is only mildly impaired, give him/her warm drinks. Then, get the victim into warm clothes and a warm sleeping bag. Place well-wrapped water bottles filled with heated water close to the victim.
- If the victim is badly impaired, attempt to keep him/her awake. Put the victim in a sleeping bag with another person—both naked. If you have a double bag, put two warm people in with the victim.

Desert Hiking

Carlsbad Caverns and Guadalupe Mountains National Parks are part of the Chihuahuan Desert. The high country of the Guadalupes is technically in another biome, but there is still desert hiking to get there and back, so prepare for the desert environment. That means having the right equipment and clothing, but it also means being mentally prepared.

For starters you should make one major mental adjustment. The only water you will ever drink in the desert is the water you carry with you. That differs significantly from most other hiking areas, where you can bank on getting water from a stream or lake and purifying or filtering it to make it safe to drink.

This is actually a difficult attitude adjustment for many people accustomed to hiking in non-desert climates, especially on their first trip to the desert. It won't be long, however, before the special character of the desert creeps into your body and takes root; then you will love the place, no matter how hot and dry it is.

Most hiking in northern climates occurs during the summer months, particularly July and August. This might be the worst time to go to the desert. The best time is either the spring (March, April, or May), when the fabulous desert wildflowers bloom, or the fall (September, October, or November), when the fall foliage is out in full color. Also, the spring and fall temperatures usually drop to a level to make hiking much more enjoyable than in the summer months.

Hiking in the desert is, simply put, more exercise. It's also more limited by the hiker's physical strength and stamina than hiking in moist climates. You really can't go lightweight because you need to carry your own water.

Experts recommend taking one gallon of water per person per day. For many people this essentially limits the length of the trip to two or three nights. A gallon of water weighs about eight pounds, so on a three-day trip (two nights out), for example, each hiker would have to carry at least twenty pounds of water.

If you're planning a longer trip and the weight of your pack is stretching your physical abilities, cut out weight in other ways instead of reducing water supply. For example, abandon optional equipment like extra camera gear or binoculars—or at least take lightweight models. Take fewer clothes—it won't kill you to wear the same shirt two days in a row. Shop for a super-lightweight tent and sleeping bag. Go with the lighter but perhaps less comfortable sleeping pad.

It might be tempting to leave your tent home to save weight, but a tent can be a lifesaver if bad weather blows in. However, you can take a lightweight, three-season tent to save weight, or you can substitute a lightweight four-person tent instead of taking two smaller tents that together weigh more.

Food presents a special challenge. The lightest foods of all (freeze-dried meals or dehydrated foods like pasta, rice, and oatmeal) require water to prepare. This means you have to add to your water supply or use alternative foods that don't require extra water.

This might seem like heresy to backpacking gourmands, but one alternative is to take the no-cooking option. Prepare evening meals in leakproof containers or make sandwiches. Plan on snacking for breakfast and lunch. This essentially means snacking all the time instead of cooking. This might seem radical, but you can save weight in two ways—less water and less gas for your stove. You could even leave your stove and gas at home if you're sure of the weather forecast and have no chance of running into cold weather.

Although the lack of water presents the biggest challenge for the hiker, the abundance of sunshine also requires special preparation and planning. Two pieces of equipment that might be optional elsewhere, sunglasses and sunscreen, are essential for desert hiking.

Don't underestimate the power of the desert sun. You might think you have a tan and don't need sunscreen, but you're probably wrong. You'll be unpleasantly shocked at how fast you can burn, and a bad sunburn, besides being unhealthy for

Watch out for the Western diamondback rattlesnake, found in both parks. The rattlesnake is a key part of the natural system. NPS PHOTO BY B. WAUER.

other reasons, will certainly take the fun out of the rest of your vacation. To be safe, use sunscreen in the 25-to-50 SPF range, and don't forget a large-brimmed hat or cap for extra protection from the sun.

Also, pay attention to the type of clothing you wear. Go "light and white," and try for natural fibers like cotton whenever possible. Even though it's better to wear long pants and a long-sleeved shirt to cut down the amount of skin exposed to the sun, many people prefer the comfort of shorts and short sleeves.

The sun isn't the only reason to wear long pants. If you're going cross-country or on a rough trail like the Blue Ridge loop in the Guadalupes or the Slaughter Canyon in Carlsbad Caverns, you definitely should wear long pants. If you don't, sotol, catclaw, cholla, and other desert flora (most species armed with spines) will be constantly taking little nicks out of your legs. Your wounds will eventually heal, but wearing long pants will be less painful. For example, lechuguilla, a knife-sharp agave, can penetrate the skin and leave a spine that can be very difficult to remove.

Although both parks have rattlesnakes, most hikers rarely see one. During the day in the summer and in winter, they usually hide away under rocks and in cracks and crevices. You're most likely to find a rattlesnake on summer evenings. Most rattlesnakes

Turkey vultures are common in both parks. NPS PHOTO.

are not aggressive and will not strike unless stepped on or provoked. If you don't hike at night and don't stick your hands or feet in crevices and under ledges, you probably won't get bitten. If you do see a rattlesnake, stay clear and don't harm it.

Another piece of equipment essential for enjoying the desert is good footwear. You don't need the extra-heavy boots mountain climbers wear, but you need sturdy boots of at least ankle height. Running or cross-training shoes might suffice for easier trips, but anything long and rough calls for sturdier boots, even more so than forested hiking areas in northern mountain ranges.

To enjoy desert hiking even more, take advantage of the early morning or late evening. The desert light is the purest early and late in the day, and usually the temperature drops to a more tolerable level. Plus, you stand a better chance of seeing desert wildlife. Most desert fauna is nocturnal, and even diurnal species usually remain inactive at midday.

Hiker's Checklist

Hiking Equipment: Equipment does not have to be new or fancy (or expensive), but make sure you test everything before you leave home.

Equipment Checklist for Day Hiking in the Desert:
    day pack or fanny pack
    water bottles
    compass
    maps
    toilet trowel
    toilet paper
    sunblock and lip lotion
    binoculars (optional)
    camera and extra film (optional)
    flashlight and extra batteries
    pocketknife and tweezers
    sunglasses
    survival kit
    first-aid kit

Added Equipment for Overnight Trips in the Desert:
    tent and waterproof fly
    sleeping bag (twenty degrees or warmer) and stuff sack
    sleeping pad
    cooking pots and pot holder
    extra water bottles
    full-size backpack
    cup, bowl, and eating utensils
    lightweight camp stove and adequate fuel
    garbage sacks
    ziplock bags
    paper towels (optional)
    nylon cord (50 ft.)
    small towel
    personal toilet kit
    notebook and pencil (optional)

Beyond the gear you'll need for hiking in the desert, you'll need some special equipment for exploring the cave routes in Carlsbad Caverns National Park.
    powerful flashlight
    backup flashlight
    two sets of extra batteries
    sweatshirt or light coat
    shoes with good grips
    knee pads and elbow pads
    long-sleeved shirt
    long pants

Clothing: In general, strive for natural fibers such as cotton and wool with earth-toned instead of bright colors. Dig around in the closet for something dull. Your wilderness partners will appreciate it. Try out the clothing before leaving home to make sure everything fits loosely with no chafing. In particular, make sure your boots are broken in, lest they break you on the first day of the hike.

Clothing for Day Hiking in the Desert:
  large-brimmed hat or cap
  sturdy hiking boots
  light, natural fiber socks
  lightweight, light-colored hiking shorts or long pants
  light-colored, long-sleeve shirt
  lightweight, windproof coat
  rain gear
  mittens or gloves (optional)

Added Clothing for Overnight Trips in the Desert:
  warm hat (e.g., stocking cap)
  long underwear
  water-resistant, windproof wilderness coat
  sweater and/or insulated vest
  long pants
  one pair of socks for each day, plus one extra pair
  underwear
  extra shirts
  sandals or lightweight shoes for wearing in camp

Food: For day hiking, bring high-energy snacks such as raisins or granola bars for lunching along the way. For overnight trips, bring enough food, including high-energy snacks, for lunching during the day, but don't overburden yourself with too much food. Plan meals carefully, bringing just enough food, plus some emergency rations. Freeze-dried foods are the lightest and safest, but they're expensive, require extra water, and aren't really necessary. Don't forget hot and cold drinks. Try to minimize food that requires extra water to prepare.

Water: With no available water sources in either Carlsbad Caverns or Guadalupe Mountains National Parks, water becomes the most critical piece of equipment on your checklist. To be safe, take one gallon per person per day (twenty-four hours). Don't drink too much of your water early in your trip, but at the same time, drink adequately and steadily throughout the day to avoid dehydration.

Map Legend

═══62═══	U.S. highway
──137──	State highway
──410──	Other road
= = = = =	Unimproved road
▬▬▬▬▬	Featured trail
- - - - - - -	Other trail
• • • • • • •	Nature trail
♠	Cabin/lodge
△	Campground
∧	Cave entrance/grotto
▲	Peak/elevation
☷	Picnic area
⬕	Ranger station
⬓	Restroom
⬚	Ruin
℘	Spring
🚶	Trailhead
❓	Visitor Center
🏇	Equestrian (Horse) Trail
⬤	Amphitheater
■	Structure

Carlsbad Caverns National Park

arlsbad Caverns National Park lies in the northern reaches of the Capitan Reef, the world's largest exposed fossil reef, named for the prominent landmark El Capitan at the southern end. The park not only hosts the famous Carlsbad Cavern, but it has 105 other caves, most with no (or limited) public access. And on top of that—literally—the park has 46,755 surface acres with about 50 miles of backcountry trails.

Carlsbad Caverns is certainly one of the treasures of the national park system. Obviously many people agree, because hordes come to see the cave each summer. And the National Park Service has offered up the wonders of Carlsbad Caverns on a silver platter. With elevators, beautifully contoured paths, detailed interpretive displays, and rangers anxious to answer all your questions, the NPS spreads out the story of Carlsbad Caverns for all to enjoy.

And compared to most other national parks, it can be an inexpensive vacation. The entrance fee is only $3.00 (age sixteen and older), and it's good for seven days.

At Carlsbad Cavern you can enjoy the depths of the cave in two distinctly different ways. You can go the mainstream tourist route and take one of the self-guided tours or you can get down and dirty and take a guided tour of what is, in essence, "an underground trail" that leaves you with the sense of what it must have been like for that first person who entered the cave with a torch or kerosene lantern. In some cases it can also leave you as dirty as a mud wrestler, so wear old clothes.

After experiencing the cave, however, you still have not seen all that Carlsbad Caverns National Park has to offer. You shouldn't leave the park without hiking below *and* above the surface.

Besides the obvious contrast between surface and subsurface, there is another big difference. The subterranean routes are elbow to elbow in the busy summer season, while up on the surface the trails are deserted. You can hike all day in gorgeous desert environs and perhaps not see another hiker—certainly a rarity in America's ultra-popular national park system.

This is the first guidebook to the trails of Carlsbad Caverns National Park, and its first edition wasn't published until 1996. Once you get out there on these trails, you'll find that fact pretty incredible.

Getting to Carlsbad Caverns National Park

From El Paso, Texas, drive northeast 142 miles on U.S. Highway 62/180 to Whites City, New Mexico. At Whites City, turn west and go 7 miles on a paved park road that dead-ends at the park headquarters, where you'll also find a visitor center, cafe, gift shop, bookstore, the Bat Flight Amphitheater, and the cave entrance. From Carlsbad, New Mexico, drive south 20 miles on US 62/180 to Whites City, then west to the park headquarters. If you're flying in and renting a car, it's best to use the El Paso airport. All services (gas station, grocery store, restaurants, motels, etc.) are available at Whites City.

Surface Routes

Most people go to Carlsbad Caverns National Park to take the cave routes, but the National Park Service has also mapped out a network of surface routes to provide a spectacular desert hiking experience. While most park visitors head to the caves, you might have the scenic trails all to yourself in many cases.

1 Chihuahuan Desert Nature Trail

Highlights: A short, self-guided interpretive trail.
Start: The Bat Flight Amphitheater at park headquarters.
Distance: 0.5-mile loop.
Difficulty: Easy.

Maps: Trails Illustrated: Carlsbad Caverns; USGS: Carlsbad Caverns.
Trail contact: Carlsbad Caverns National Park, 3225 National Park Highway, Carlsbad, NM 88220; (505) 785-2232; www.nps.gov/cave.

Finding the trailhead: Park in the visitor center parking lot. The trail starts either at the west end of the parking lot or at the Bat Flight Amphitheater.

The Hike

This trail is for everybody. It's partially paved, has lots of interesting interpretation, and is accessible to people with mobility impairments. You can take the short loop in either direction, but the interpretive signs are set up in a counterclockwise sequence. There are benches for relaxing along the way. At one stop, about halfway around, you get a expansive view of the desert basin to the southeast.

If you plan to watch the grand exit of bats from Carlsbad or if you plan to visit the cave, plan on getting to the headquarters area a half-hour early and take a leisurely stroll around this trail first. The trail is closed during the bat flight to avoid disturbing the bats.

The interpretive signs along the trail give you a great introduction to desert flora and how native cultures used desert plants. You can learn how early residents roasted sotol hearts, wove diapers from juniper bark and rope from lechuguilla leaves, made cough medicine from ocotillo, and smashed soap from the roots of the Torrey yucca. You can also see why they called the Torrey yucca the "Spanish dagger" and, just as obviously, how the catclaw acacia earned its name.

About halfway around the half-mile trail, you can see a fenced-off area protecting a second natural entrance to the caverns. Just east of the fenced-off area (not accessible by trail) lie two shafts blasted into the bat cave. Guano miners created these artificial entrances (now sealed) to more easily remove the guano, but it turned

Chihuahuan Desert Nature Trail

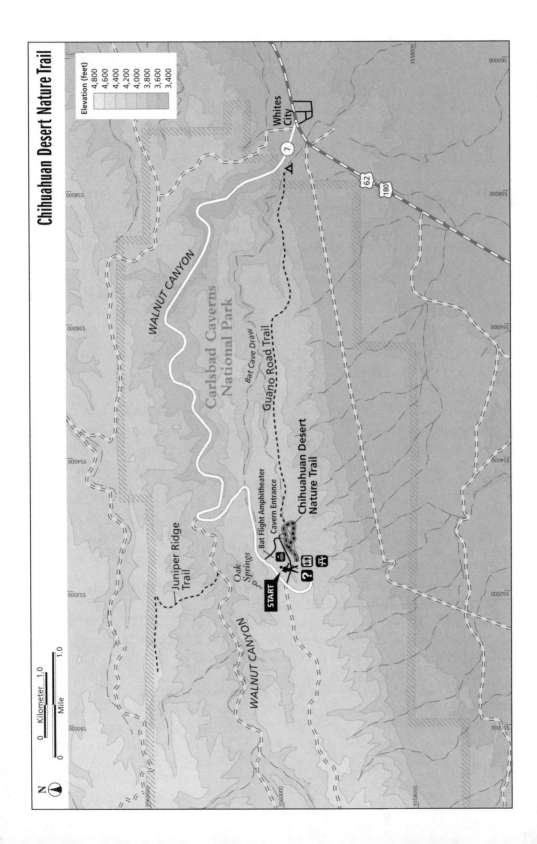

The Chihuahuan Desert Nature Trail with the Carlsbad Caverns visitor center and the Bat Flight Amphitheater in the background.

out to be self-defeating. The artificial entrances upset the delicate habitat used for centuries by the bats. The end result was, regrettably and ironically, a reduced bat population and, of course, less guano.

2 Guano Road Trail

Highlights: A pleasant stroll through the desert environment on a historic route used by guano miners in the 1900s.
Start: The Bat Flight Amphitheater at park headquarters or at the west end of the campground at Whites City.
Distance: 3.5-mile shuttle.

Difficulty: Easy.
Maps: Trails Illustrated: Carlsbad Caverns; USGS: Carlsbad Caverns.
Trail contact: Carlsbad Caverns National Park, 3225 National Park Highway, Carlsbad, NM 88220; (505) 785–2232; www.nps.gov/cave.

Finding the trailhead: The trailhead at the park headquarters is easy to find. The trail starts right at the Bat Flight Amphitheater where the Chihuahuan Desert Nature Trail ends. In fact, the first 0.25 mile is also part of the Chihuahuan Desert Nature Trail. However, the trailhead at

The beginning of the Guano Road Trail at the west end of Whites City.

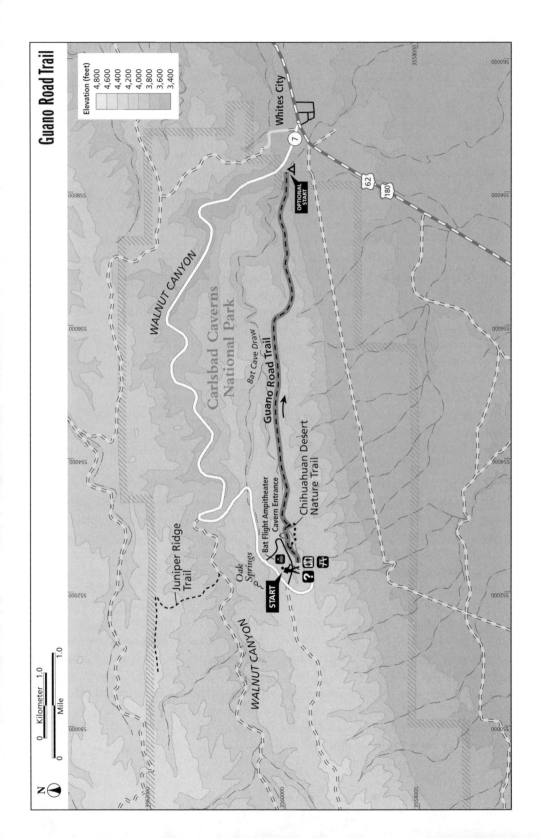

Guano Road Trail

Elevation (feet)
- 4,800
- 4,600
- 4,400
- 4,200
- 4,000
- 3,800
- 3,600
- 3,400

Whites City

WALNUT CANYON

Carlsbad Caverns
National Park

Bat Cave Draw

Guano Road Trail

OPTIONAL
START

Chihuahuan Desert
Nature Trail

Bat Flight Ampitheater
Cavern Entrance

Juniper Ridge
Trail

Oak
Springs

START

WALNUT CANYON

62

180

7

N

0   Kilometer   1.0

0   Mile   1.0

Whites City is not as easy to find. The trail starts at the westernmost part of a private camp-ground on the west end of Whites City. Watch for a new sign at the Whites City trailhead. You can also easily see what looks like an old jeep road heading up the hill from the campground. That's the trail.

The Hike

This might be the most convenient way to experience the "other" Carlsbad Caverns, the world above ground. This trail follows the ridge just south of the paved road from Whites City to the park headquarters. Even though you never get far from the highway, much of the trail is out of sight and sound of the road.

You can start at either end, but for the easiest route start at the Bat Flight Amphitheater. This makes the trail a gradual downhill walk the entire way.

Since this is a shuttle, transportation can be a problem. One idea is to take your trip into the cavern and then, instead of your entire party driving down to Whites City, somebody can volunteer to drive down, allowing the rest of your group to take a great desert hike and warm up after the coolish visit to the depths of Carlsbad Cavern. If you're early for your cave trip, you can do this in reverse. One person can drive up to the headquarters while the rest of the party hikes up from Whites City.

From a geologist's perspective this trail starts at the base of the Capitan Reef and climbs to the top, where the caverns are located. From a hiker's perspective it's an extra-pleasant stroll through a desert environment.

From the west end it's a very easy hike, but even if you start at Whites City, it's not difficult. You climb for about a half mile, and then it's essentially flat the rest of the way to the amphitheater. Shortly up the trail from the Whites City Camp-ground, you find a "walk only" gate to keep out motorized vehicles.

The trail is well defined and easy to follow all the way with the exception of the uphill section at the east end. Here the trail fades away in the rocks here and there, but you can find your way by following cairns and brown trail markers placed in strategic locations by the National Park Service.

From the top of the ridge, you get a good view of tiny Whites City below and the "great flat" beyond. Along the trail you also get to see much of the desert vege-tation you may have read about on the interpretive signs along the Chihuahuan Desert Nature Trail.

This trail traces the same route used by guano miners in the early 1900s to haul the prized fertilizer to Whites City in wagons. You can still see signs of the past, as two wagon tracks are visible much of the way. You can also see a few pieces of aban-doned mining equipment rusting away along the abandoned road. Please do not remove any of this "garbage" left by guano miners. These historical artifacts have lit-tle value when removed, and in their current location they become part of the fas-cinating story of guano mining. Preserve this story for other hikers to follow. (And besides, it's illegal to remove them from the park.)

3 Juniper Ridge

Highlights: A convenient short hike, ideal for your afternoon after your morning trip into the cave.
Start: 1 mile past marker 15 on Scenic Loop Drive.
Distance: 2 to 4 miles out and back.
Difficulty: Easy.
Maps: Trails Illustrated: Carlsbad Caverns; USGS: Carlsbad Caverns.
Trail contact: Carlsbad Caverns National Park, 3225 National Park Highway, Carlsbad, NM 88220; (505) 785-2232; www.nps.gov/cave.

Finding the trailhead: The only difficult part of this trail is finding it. Take the Scenic Loop Drive turnout off the paved road to park headquarters, just east of the visitor center. You must be careful not to miss it, because you can't turn around and backtrack on this one-way road.

This trail used to be called North Boundary Trail, so if you see any old handouts or signs, they actually refer to the Juniper Ridge Trail. The National Park Service handout might say the trail starts "just past" marker 15 on Scenic Loop Drive, but it actually starts about 1 mile past marker 15, almost to marker 16. There's no parking area at the trailhead. Set your odometer at marker 15 and go about 0.9 mile until you see a pullout on the north side of the road. Park here and walk about 200 yards up the road until you see the trail heading off to the north. If you see marker 16, park and walk back down the road to the trailhead. Watch for a sign at the trailhead as well as a faint trail and a string of cairns heading north from the road.

The Hike

This is an ideal short hike to take during your afternoon drive around Scenic Loop Drive, perhaps after your visit to the cave earlier that morning. Unlike most other hikes in the park, however, the trail to the north boundary does not follow a canyon bottom. Instead, it's a short walk in the desert and serves as a good introduction to desert hiking.

Another good plan is to take this hike early in the morning before the desert heats up. This gives you a better chance to see wildlife and the gorgeous morning light highlighting the desert landscape. Then, about the time the sun is bearing down hard, you can head for the cool depths of the cave.

The trail is fairly easy to follow. It's well defined in some places, not in others, but in all cases well-placed cairns show the way. With a few small switchbacks, the trail heads north up a moderately steep upgrade for about a mile up to the fence line that marks the park boundary.

You can turn back here, making the total distance about 2 miles, and this is the official end of the trail. However, you can stretch the hike out to about 4 miles by following the fence line for a while. You can go either left or right, but make a mental picture of the spot where the trail meets the fence line.

The cairns continue along the fence line up to a mile in each direction. When cairns start to get scarce and hard to see, turn back. When you head back, be careful

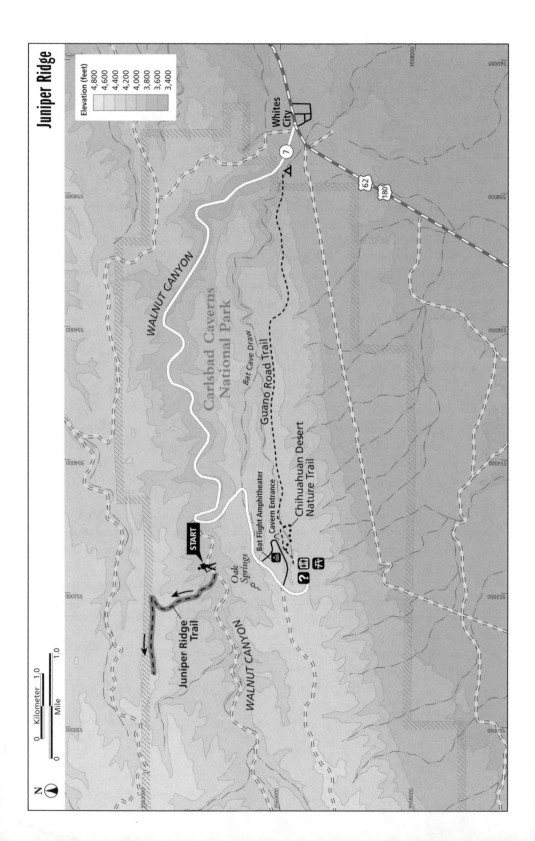

Juniper Ridge

you don't walk right by the trail going south to the trailhead and continue following cairns along the boundary. This is actually easy to do since much of the terrain is strikingly similar.

This trail offers a good opportunity to sample the park's wildflowers and other vegetation and to see wildlife, especially on early-morning walks. On the way back you get a nice view into the expansive Walnut Canyon, formed by the powerful flash floods that roar down the canyon once every two or three years. You can also see the canyon's namesake, undersized walnut trees, lining the streambed.

4 Rattlesnake Canyon

Highlights: A trip into the more remote sections of the park suited for an overnighter for those who want to spend the night out.
Start: Marker 9 on Scenic Loop Drive.
Distance: 7 miles (out and back) or 5 miles (loop).

Difficulty: Moderate.
Maps: Trails Illustrated: Carlsbad Caverns; USGS: Serpentine Bends.
Trail contact: Carlsbad Caverns National Park, 3225 National Park Highway, Carlsbad, NM 88220; (505) 785-2232; www.nps.gov/cave.

Finding the trailhead: The trail starts at marker 9 on Scenic Loop Drive, a well-maintained gravel road that leaves the paved entrance road to the park just east of the visitor center. This is a one-way road, so careful not to be taken in by the scenery and miss marker 9, as you'll have to drive all the way around again to get to the trailhead. There's room to park three or four vehicles at marker 9.

The Hike

This is definitely one of the most scenic and accessible trails in Carlsbad Caverns. Yet as with most other surface trails in the park, you're likely to have the trail all to yourself. Rattlesnake Canyon is a large, open valley where you can quietly soak in the true essence of the Chihuahuan Desert and the rugged individuality of its plants and animals. If you plan to take a cave route, consider getting up early and hiking Rattlesnake Canyon when the temperature is lower and the wildlife is out in force. Then visit the cave in the afternoon.

When hiking Rattlesnake Canyon, you have two options. You can follow the canyon out to the park boundary and return to the trailhead, or you can take a small loop by connecting with the Guadalupe Ridge Trail and following it back to Scenic Loop Drive, coming out about a mile up the road from the Rattlesnake Canyon trailhead. If you opt for the loop option and have two vehicles in your party, leave one at the Guadalupe Ridge trailhead.

Both the loop and the out-and-back trip make excellent day hikes, but you can also make Rattlesnake Canyon an overnight trip. You can, of course, do this loop in reverse, but this description describes the clockwise route.

Cairns are all that mark parts of the Rattlesnake Canyon Trail.

At the beginning the trail is slightly confusing. From the parking area it goes off to the right and down a short, steep hill to the bottom of the canyon. Then it climbs briefly and traverses the left side of a small canyon for a short way. The first part of the trail is well defined and easy to follow. Then it drops down into the bottom of Rattlesnake Canyon and alternates between short sections of trail and stretches of dry wash with cairns showing the way. After the short descent into the bottom of the canyon, the trail remains fairly level the rest of the way.

Rattlesnake is a wide-open and more vegetatively diverse canyon than others in the park. Some of the broad, flat benches are almost like grassland. There's lots of deer food—and lots of deer.

About 1.5 miles into Rattlesnake Canyon, you hit a signed junction. The loop trail (marked GUADALUPE RIDGE) veers off to the right and heads west up North Rattlesnake Canyon and then north over a small ridge and down to the Guadalupe Ridge Trail. This recently opened trail is defined most of the way with cairns marking the sections where the trail gets faint.

You can also hike straight along the canyon (marked STONE RANCH) for about 2 miles to the park boundary and return to the trailhead. Just past the point where the

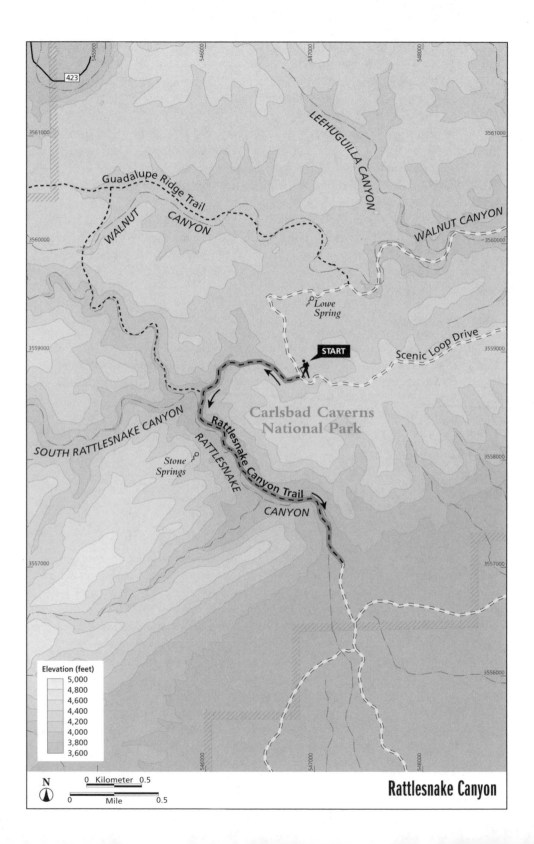

Rattlesnake Canyon

new trail heads up to Guadalupe Ridge, you pass through historic Stone Ranch. Stone Springs (up the hill to the right) provided water for an early-1900s ranch in Rattlesnake Canyon. You can scramble up to see the springs, but it's a steep climb. You can see some old evidence of the ranching operations at both the springs and in the canyon along the trail.

If you plan to stay overnight, try to find a good campsite somewhere along the canyon floor, perhaps on one of the delightful grassy benches that line the lower canyon south of Stone Ranch. After a pleasant night in the desert, you can take the short hike back to the trailhead or the loop route. The elevation gain back to the trailhead on both routes is about the same.

To take the loop option, go right when you intersect with the Guadalupe Ridge Trail and hike gradually downhill along Walnut Canyon for about 2 miles to Scenic Loop Drive. If you don't have a shuttle vehicle at the end of the hike, somebody will have to volunteer to hike the extra mile along Scenic Loop Drive to the Rattlesnake Canyon trailhead to get your vehicle.

Miles and Directions

0.0 Start at the trailhead located at marker 9 on Scenic Loop Drive.

1.5 At the junction with the trail to Guadalupe Ridge, turn left for an out and back. **Option:** For a loop, turn right at this junction and hike downhill along Walnut Canyon for about 2 miles back to Scenic Loop Drive.

1.7 Arrive at Stone Ranch and pass Stone Springs.

3.5 Reach the park boundary.

5 Guadalupe Ridge

Highlights: A long route through the heart of the park, but hikers have the option of doing only part of it.
Start: The well-marked trailhead on Scenic Loop Drive.
Distance: Up to 23.6 miles out and back.
Difficulty: Easy to difficult, depending on the distance.

Maps: Trails Illustrated: Carlsbad Caverns; USGS: Serpentine Bends, Gunsight Canyon, and Queen.
Trail contact: Carlsbad Caverns National Park, 3225 National Park Highway, Carlsbad, NM 88220; (505) 785-2232; www.nps.gov/cave.

Finding the trailhead: The trail starts about halfway around Scenic Loop Drive, a well-maintained gravel road that leaves the paved entrance road to the park just east of the visitor center. This is a one-way road, so be careful not to miss the sign that says GUADALUPE RIDGE TRAIL. Park here.

The Hike

The Guadalupe Ridge Trail is the center stage of the Carlsbad Caverns trail system. From this trail you can see most of the park and get a great feeling for the expansiveness and beauty of Carlsbad Caverns above the surface. Since the Guadalupe Ridge Trail is an abandoned jeep road, the National Park Service allows mountain biking. However, mountain biking off this trail is strictly prohibited, either cross-country or on connecting trails down Rattlesnake and Slaughter Canyons.

As with all desert hiking, it's best to go early. Walnut Canyon is always a grand place to hike, but it's even better at first light. You're likely to see deer and other desert wildlife during the first hours of daylight.

The first 3 miles follow Walnut Canyon and is easy walking. You go through two gates, as the trail goes out of and then, 0.5 mile later, back into the park. The public has legal access to this Bureau of Land Management land, but be sure to close the gates. You cross the usually dry streambed of Walnut Creek just after the second gate.

Walnut is bigger and more open than most canyons in the park. Watch for wildlife, which is abundant, especially a healthy population of mule deer. Golden eagles often soar through the canyon looking for a black-tailed jackrabbit for dinner. And if you're out at daybreak, you might see a ringtail. Also, the wildflower show is sensational along the first section of the trail.

Right after the second gate the trail heads up a steep hill and keeps climbing for about 3 miles until you reach the top of the ridge. From that point on you face only small ups and downs, and the trail stays essentially level or slightly uphill to the west boundary and Putnam Cabin.

Although it's a healthy climb to get to the top of the ridge, it's still easier than going up Slaughter Canyon or Yucca Canyon Trail to reach the same elevation. The

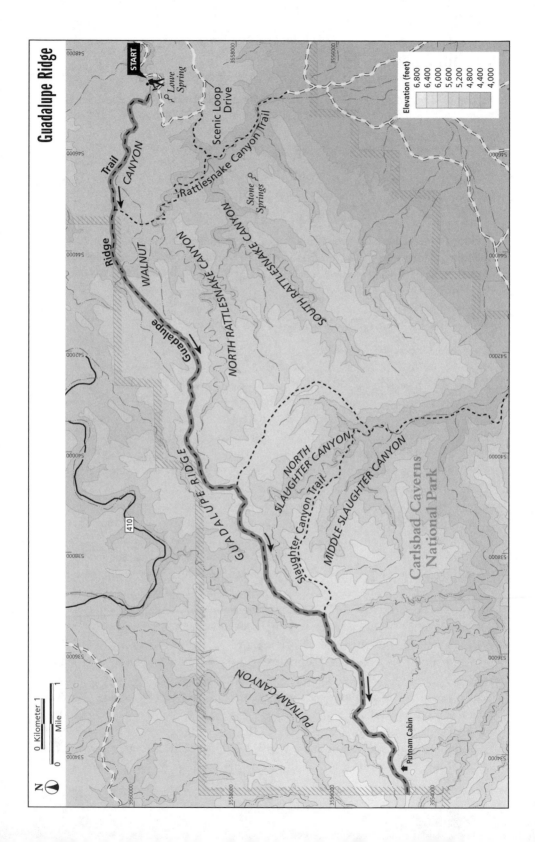

Guadalupe Ridge

Elevation (feet)
6,800
6,400
6,000
5,600
5,200
4,800
4,400
4,000

START

Louve Spring

Scenic Loop Drive

Rattlesnake Canyon Trail

Stone Springs

CANYON

Trail

Ridge

WALNUT CANYON

Guadalupe

NORTH RATTLESNAKE CANYON

SOUTH RATTLESNAKE CANYON

GUADALUPE RIDGE

410

NORTH SLAUGHTER CANYON

Slaughter Canyon Trail

MIDDLE SLAUGHTER CANYON

Carlsbad Caverns National Park

PUTNAM CANYON

Putnam Cabin

N

0   Kilometer 1

0   Mile   1

trail, which is an unmaintained jeep road, is much easier to walk than most trails. You can spend your time gazing at the spectacular scenery instead of making sure you have the next cairn spotted. If you want to make good time, you're on the right trail. You can average 2 to 3 mph on this trail, whereas you are hard-pressed to do 1.5 mph on most park trails.

This trail offers a variety of hiking. If you're out for a pleasant early-morning or late-evening stroll, you can walk all or part of the first 3 miles and return to your vehicle. If you want to stay out one or two nights, you're also on the right trail. Once you get to the top of the ridge, you'll find several excellent places to camp. Probably the best camping areas are in a juniper grove around the junction with Slaughter Canyon Trail, which heads off to the west at about the 9.5-mile mark.

From the ridge you see some of the best scenery in the park. This could be called "reef-walking," as you're right on top of the 250-million-year-old Capitan Reef. There's no El Capitan or Grand Teton or Longs Peak around to dominate the landscape. Instead, you look down in one canyon after another as they end near the ridgeline.

When I hiked this route, you could see Putnam Cabin and its big antenna a long way off sitting on top of a high point on the ridge. The cabin wasn't the stereotypical old log cabin you might visualize when you look at the map, but it had an outdoor toilet you could use. However, the NPS plans to remove the cabin (and toilet) in the next few years, so it might be gone when you get there.

If you're retracing your steps on the ridge, you can see Carlsbad Caverns Visitor Center many miles away, but you don't have to walk quite that far. The last few miles back to the visitor center are part of Scenic Loop Drive.

You can also make this a shuttle hike by leaving a vehicle or arranging to be picked up at the Slaughter Canyon trailhead. If you take this option, you don't have to retrace your steps to Scenic Loop Drive. And you can drop your pack and take a short side-trip over to Putnam Cabin and the west boundary before heading down Slaughter Canyon.

You can reach Slaughter Canyon trailhead on two different trails. The first option (signed junction at the 7-mile mark) goes along Slaughter Ridge before steeply dropping into broad and beautiful Slaughter Canyon. The second route (signed junction at the 9.5-mile mark) follows the ridge between North and Middle Slaughter Canyons for about 1.5 miles before dropping (not quite as steeply) into the canyon bottom.

Miles and Directions

0.0   Start at the GUADALUPE RIDGE TRAIL sign located halfway around Scenic Loop Drive.

2.0   At the Rattlesnake Canyon Trail junction, turn right.

2.5   Pass the first gate.

2.9   Cross the Walnut Creek dry wash.

3.0 Pass the second gate.

7.0 At the Slaughter Ridge Trail junction, turn right.

9.5 At the next Slaughter Canyon Trail junction, turn right.

11.7 Arrive at Putnam Cabin.

11.8 Reach the park boundary. Turn around and head back to the trailhead.

6 Slaughter Canyon

Highlights: A long route suited for a desert backpacking adventure, but you can turn around at any point to make it a shorter hike.
Start: Parking lot for Slaughter Canyon Cave (may be called New Cave in older publications).
Distance: 11 miles out and back, with a shuttle option.

Difficulty: Difficult.
Maps: Trails Illustrated: Carlsbad Caverns; USGS: Serpentine Bends and Grapevine Draw.
Trail contact: Carlsbad Caverns National Park, 3225 National Park Highway, Carlsbad, NM 88220; (505) 785-2232; www.nps.gov/cave.

Finding the trailhead: The paved road to Slaughter Canyon Cave (County Road 418) turns off U.S. Highway 62/180, 6 miles south of Whites City. The signs at the turnoff say SLAUGHTER CANYON CAVE and WASHINGTON RANCH. Follow CR 418 for 10 miles until you reach the park boundary and the road turns to gravel. Follow the gravel road for another mile until it dead-ends at the trailhead. There is plenty of parking at the trailhead, which also has toilet and picnic facilities.

The Hike

Slaughter Canyon is a broad desert canyon with three major branches—West, Middle, and North. Get out the long pants for this trail. It gets brushy, and your desert friends—catclaw, sotol, cholla, and their thorny relatives—can torture bare legs. Be sure to bring your own water because you won't find any at the trailhead.

Slaughter Canyon offers many options. It can be a leisurely day hike of 2 to 3 miles up the fairly level canyon and then returning to the trailhead, or you can make it a fitness test by tackling the entire 11 miles in a single day.

However, Slaughter Canyon is probably best suited to a backpacking adventure with one or two nights out in the remote desert wilderness. You can also make this part of a long shuttle hike by starting at the Guadalupe Ridge trailhead on Scenic Loop Drive and ending at the Slaughter Canyon trailhead.

Two trails leave from this trailhead, so the first order of business is to make sure you're on the right one. Don't take the left-hand trail to Slaughter Canyon Cave, which is more heavily used and defined than the Slaughter Canyon Trail. The correct trail is just to the right of the cave trail. The sign at the trailhead refers to the trail as the MIDDLE SLAUGHTER CANYON TRAIL. The cave trail immediately starts climbing, and the canyon trail stays low and follows the dry wash.

Slaughter Canyon Trail.

The trail starts out on a beautiful grassy bench and then winds in and out of the canyon wash. Watch carefully for cairns along this stretch, as it's easy to miss them in places. A few sections of the trail don't have enough cairns, but don't fret. The trail continues up the canyon wash. If you stay in the canyon wash, you'll get to the same place as the trail goes, but staying on the trail is easier on the feet and makes the trip slightly shorter, as it cuts across some of the meanders.

You might see spur trails heading off to the left or right. Ignore these and keep heading up the main canyon. About 1.5 miles up the trail, you can see West Slaughter Canyon heading off to the left. The gradual incline up Slaughter Canyon continues for 3 miles, at which point the trail starts climbing up to a ridge between North Slaughter Canyon and Middle Slaughter Canyon.

After you start climbing the hiking becomes more difficult, especially with an overnight pack. It's steep, and the trail fades away in a few places where you must follow well-placed cairns. After a tough mile the steep climb is behind you and you hike on a fairly level trail along the ridge. The vistas from the ridgeline are fantastic.

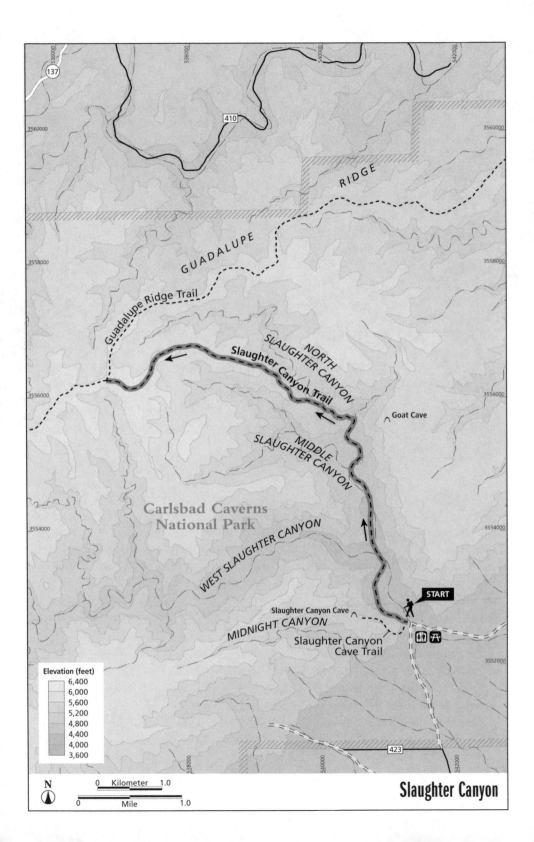

137

410

RIDGE

GUADALUPE

Guadalupe Ridge Trail

Guadalupe Ridge Trail

NORTH SLAUGHTER CANYON

Slaughter Canyon Trail

Goat Cave

MIDDLE SLAUGHTER CANYON

Carlsbad Caverns
National Park

WEST SLAUGHTER CANYON

START

Slaughter Canyon Cave

MIDNIGHT CANYON

Slaughter Canyon
Cave Trail

423

Elevation (feet)

6,400
6,000
5,600
5,200
4,800
4,400
4,000
3,600

N

0   Kilometer   1.0

0   Mile   1.0

Slaughter Canyon

When you reach the Guadalupe Ridge Trail, take a long break before heading back down the ridge to the trailhead.

Miles and Directions

0.0   Start at the trailhead and follow the right-hand trail with the MIDDLE SLAUGHTER CANYON TRAIL sign.

1.5   Pass West Slaughter Canyon.

3.0   At the junction with Slaughter Canyon Trail, turn left.

5.5   Reach the Guadalupe Ridge Trail (your turnaround point).

8.0   At the junction with Slaughter Canyon Trail, turn right.

11.0   Arrive at the Slaughter Canyon trailhead.

7 Yucca Canyon

Highlights: Perhaps the most austere and scenic hiking route in the park.
Start: Yucca Canyon trailhead.
Distance: 7 miles out and back to the top of Yucca Canyon, 12 miles out and back to the head of Double Canyon.

Difficulty: Difficult.
Maps: Trails Illustrated: Carlsbad Caverns; USGS: Grapevine Draw and Gunsight Canyon.
Trail contact: Carlsbad Caverns National Park, 3225 National Park Highway, Carlsbad, NM 88220; (505) 785–2232; www.nps.gov/cave.

Finding the trailhead: The paved road to the Yucca Canyon trailhead (County Road 418) turns off U.S. Highway 62/180, 6 miles south of Whites City. The signs at the turnoff say SLAUGHTER CANYON CAVE and WASHINGTON RANCH. Follow CR 418 for 10 miles until you reach the park boundary and the road turns to gravel. At this point turn left (west) onto a rough gravel road that follows the north side of the fence line. Stay on this road for 1.7 miles until it ends at the Yucca Canyon trailhead. You should have a high-clearance vehicle, preferably four-wheel drive, for the last 1.7 miles.

The Hike

This is perhaps the most dramatic and scenic trail in the park. It might also be the most rugged.

Yucca Canyon is suited for a long day hike or an overnighter. If you day hike, get up early and plan on getting back late. If you backpack, you can spend the night up on the ridge above Yucca Canyon. This is a special treat, but you have to earn it. It's a rough uphill grind (more than 1,500 feet in about 3.5 miles!) with an overnight pack to get there. Staying overnight gives you the time to do several splendid side-trips in the area.

Most canyon hikes in the park, such as Slaughter Canyon just to the east, at least start out with a near-level walk along the streambed, but not in this case. You start climbing right from the trailhead.

View from the top of Yucca Canyon.

This is a narrower, more scenic canyon than others in the park. The scenery is so absorbing that you might forget the steady elevation gain. The vegetation is so diverse and lush (but no more yucca than in other canyons) that you might think the canyon has a spring-fed stream, but no water is visible.

You'll also see one precipitous rock formation after another. In two places the cliffs on both sides of the canyon come together like gates.

The trail is very well constructed and defined—perhaps the best in the park. The climbing ends after about 3.5 miles when you reach the top of the escarpment and break out into a gorgeous grove of junipers with a grassy carpet, perhaps the closest thing to a forest you'll find in this park.

From here the hiking is fairly flat. Up here the trail is less defined but still easy to follow because of a steady string of cairns. The trail turns west and wanders through the junipers for about a mile. It's easy to feel lonely up here. It seems like you have a whole wilderness to yourself, and the only sounds are the wind making music as it sifts through the junipers and an occasional deer bounding away.

If you were wondering about that strange green spot on the USGS topo map, you're in it. The green generally follows the boundaries of the juniper grove. This isn't

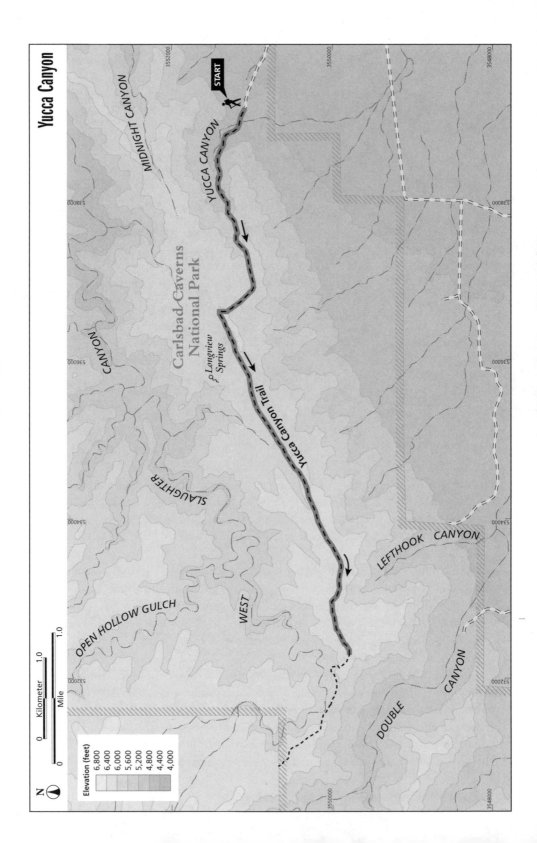

Yucca Canyon

The cliffs of Double Canyon at the end of the Yucca Canyon hike.

the only spot like this in the park, and in fact there are other spots with as much or more vegetation, but for some reason the USGS chose to highlight this juniper grove.

If you're staying overnight, you'll want to pick a choice campsite amid the junipers. You may see a fenced enclosure where the National Park Service is conducting a vegetation study.

If you're day hiking, you might want to have a long lunch in the junipers and head back. However, if you're ambitious, you can continue along the ridge overlooking Double Canyon, about another 2.5 miles (one way).

As you approach Double Canyon, the trail gets harder to find and you must rely completely on cairns in most places. But it stays level as you walk the ridgeline, and the scenery is fantastic all the way.

About a mile before Double Canyon, you can peek over the cliffs into precipitous Lefthook Canyon. Another mile down the trail gives you a similar view into the much larger Double Canyon. Both canyons veer off to the south from the ridge.

Shortly after your view over the sheer cliffs into Double Canyon, the trail takes a sharp turn to the left (south) and heads down a short hill to a saddle at the head of Double Canyon. At this point the trail more or less disappears. The USGS and Trails

Illustrated maps show the trail continuing out the west end of the park and connecting with Guadalupe Ridge several miles into the Lincoln National Forest. But on the ground the trail is barely visible, with a few scattered cairns marking the way.

If you're an ambitious and experienced hiker, you can turn left and follow a level rock ledge for about 0.5 mile. From this point you can look off to the east side of Double Canyon and see the spectacular "double cliffs" you were able to peek over when you were on the ridgeline trail a few minutes earlier. You also get a great view of expansive Double Canyon. This side-trip can be dangerous, so be careful.

After a good rest at the end of the trail, retrace your steps back to the juniper grove at the top of Yucca Canyon.

Another nice side-trip from the juniper grove at the head of Yucca Canyon is the short cross-country trip to Longview Springs. You'll need your compass and topo map, but it isn't hard to find. If you get lucky, you'll be able to follow well-defined deer trails to the spring. From the spring you definitely get a "long view" off to the west. The spring is merely a seep with not much water flow, but nonetheless it's a wonderful oasis in the desert. Don't plan on using the spring for drinking water, and be extra careful not to trample sensitive plants around the springs.

On the way back down Yucca Canyon, you'll be quickly reminded how steep it was getting up. You might have been reveling in the scenery and not noticed. It's so steep that it's hard to walk down in places.

Miles and Directions

0.0   Start at the Yucca Canyon trailhead.

3.5   Reach the top of Yucca Canyon. **Option:** Turn around here for 7-mile out and back.

4.0   Pass the turnoff to Longview Springs. **Option:** Turn right for a short cross-country trip to Longview Springs.

5.0   Pass Lefthook Canyon.

6.0   Reach the end of the trail. Turn around here for 12-mile out and back. **Option:** Continue another 2.5 miles (one way) along the ridge overlooking Double Canyon.

Cave Routes

At Carlsbad Caverns National Park, the National Park Service has put together a spectacular and diverse package of cave routes for park visitors. Park visitors can choose from eight cave routes ranging from very easy to very difficult.

It would be much easier for the NPS to herd everybody through the caverns on the self-guided tours. But instead they provide the opportunity for "wild cave experiences."

The ultra-popular self-guided tours still attract the most visitors, just as they have for decades. But in recent years the NPS has added ranger-led trips to the selection. Two of these ranger-led tours are fairly easy, but two of the cave routes are nothing short of a down-and-dirty caving experiences. Here's the lineup, listed in approximate order of difficulty:

Self-Guided Tours
  The Big Room
  Natural Entrance

Guided Tours
  King's Palace
  Lefthand Tunnel
  Lower Cave
  Slaughter Canyon Cave

Caving Experiences
  Spider Cave
  Hall of the White Giant

For all routes you definitely need good hiking shoes. Don't show up in sandals, high heels, or shoes with slick soles. Also, to really enjoy the cave, bring a good flashlight (and extra batteries). Small, weak flashlights don't allow you to clearly see the fantastic formations. Parents should carefully supervise young children, and for safety reasons the NPS does not allow strollers in the cave.

For the ranger-led caving trips, you need a special piece of equipment—courage. These trips are not for the fainthearted. They are, in fact, an introduction to the sport of caving. They also require at least a moderate level of physical fitness.

One note of caution—big people beware. Anybody the size of an NFL lineman should avoid the Spider Cave and Hall of the White Giant. On these two trips you not only get down on your belly and crawl through the mud, but you also have to squeeze through some spaces tight enough to bring out deep-rooted claustrophobic tendencies.

You also need old clothes. The NPS hands out a hard hat with a light along with knee and elbow pads at the start of the trip.

Cross Section of Carlsbad Caverns

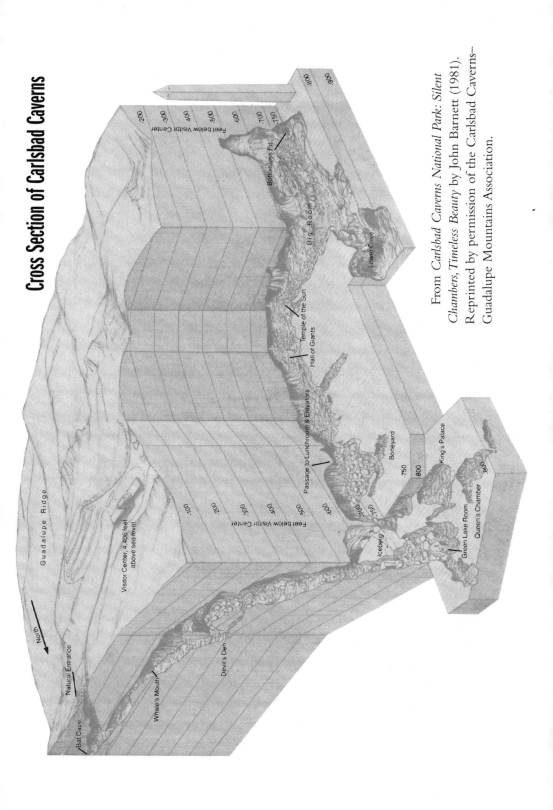

From *Carlsbad Caverns National Park: Silent Chambers, Timeless Beauty* by John Barnett (1981). Reprinted by permission of the Carlsbad Caverns–Guadalupe Mountains Association.

Because of safety concerns and the physical difficulty of the off-trail cave routes, the NPS does not allow children under age twelve on the Lower Cave, Spider Cave, and Hall of the White Giant trips. Also, people who have difficulty with low levels of light, small spaces, or heights may prefer the self-guided tours. Many parts of these off-trail trips are physically demanding, wet and slippery, have tight squeezes, and at times require hand lines (short, fixed ropes) to get up steep slopes. All off-trail tours have a special "blackout" to help visitors truly experience the natural cave.

Up on the surface the hiking is free. But the NPS charges a small fee for the cave routes. Holders of the Golden Age or Golden Access passport get a 50 percent discount on the guided tours and free access for self-guided tours. You must make reservations for all tours except the two self-guided routes. Call (800) 967–2283 for reservations, which require a Visa or MasterCard. If you are unable to keep your reservation, please cancel it twenty-four hours or more in advance for a full refund. This courtesy allows others to take these limited-participation tours.

Even though the current schedules are included in the following descriptions, be sure to call in advance and double-check, as all schedules are subject to change. As a special courtesy to rangers and others on your trip, try to arrive a few minutes early.

Necessary Equipment

- Good walking shoes—no high heels, sandals, or shoes with slick soles.
- Sweater, sweatshirt, or light coat. The cave stays at a constant temperature of fifty-six degrees Fahrenheit, and that might seem chilly compared to the ninety-plus degrees of the desert above.
- A good flashlight with extra batteries is welcome on all cave trips and required on Slaughter Cave tours.

For Everybody

For safety reasons and to preserve the cave experience for many generations to come, the NPS has a few rules for all underground routes.
- No smoking is allowed anywhere in any caves in Carlsbad Caverns National Park, including the Underground Lunch Room.
- Stay on designated trails at all times.
- Do not touch any cave formations.
- Keep children under close supervision at all times.
- Do not flash other cave visitors with your camera.
- Do not shine your flashlight into the faces of other visitors.
- No strollers are allowed anywhere in Carlsbad Caverns.
- Try to be as quiet as possible to preserve the cave experience for other visitors.
- Never throw anything in cave pools.

- Do not bring food or beverage into the caves except for bottled water, which is allowed anywhere in the cave.

8 Natural Entrance

Highlights: A self-guided trip on a paved path.
Start: Visitor center.
Distance: 1 mile out and back, plus an additional 1.2 miles if you go through the Big Room.
Difficulty: Moderate; not recommended for anybody with heart problems or walking difficulties.
Schedule: Any time between 8:30 A.M. and 3:30 P.M. daily May through August and 8:30 A.M. to 2:00 P.M. September through April. No reservations required. Buy tickets at the visitor center.
Special regulations: No strollers. Stay on cave trails at all times.
Trail contact: Carlsbad Caverns National Park, 3225 National Park Highway, Carlsbad, NM 88220; (505) 785-2232; www.nps.gov/cave.

Finding the trailhead: To find the trailhead, turn west off U.S. Highway 62/180 at Whites City (20 miles south of Carlsbad, New Mexico) and drive 7 miles on a paved road to the park headquarters and visitor center.

The Hike

Assuming you're physically ready for a steep, 2.2-mile, mostly downhill walk, the Natural Entrance route probably gets the nod as the best way to see Carlsbad Cavern. You get the spine-tingling sensation of descending seventy-five stories into the Big Room; from there you can take the Big Room route; and then you can avoid climbing back up by taking the elevator to the surface. You'll also find many excellent interpretive signs along the way to explain the story of Carlsbad Cavern.

As you leave the visitor center and start down the long, winding path to the Natural Entrance, try to imagine what it was like for those who discovered the cave. Local Indians were the first to enter the cave, but they probably did not go into its depths.

In the late 1800s local cowboys noticed "smoke" coming out of a hole in the ground. But when they went to investigate that cloud of smoke, it turned out to be clouds of bats leaving the cave at dusk. Bats still inhabit the cave, but the population has been much reduced by use of insecticides and early damage to their critical cave habitat. The bats roost in a section of the cave closed off from public access, so you probably won't see any bats on your trip into the cave. However, you might see cave swallows darting here and there around the Natural Entrance. If you want to see bats (and it's quite the spectacle!), make sure you take a seat at the Bat Flight Amphitheater at the Natural Entrance at dusk on any summer night.

After descending about 200 feet into the cave, you'll enter the "twilight zone," the mysterious region of a cave that still gets faint light from the outside world but

Heading into the Natural Entrance.

is mostly dominated by the blackness of the cavern depths. Past the twilight zone you see the cave with the help of more than 1,000 lightbulbs and 19 miles of wire, all aesthetically and carefully placed by the National Park Service to enhance the cave experience. It may seem like the NPS uses colored lights, but it actually places lights strategically to highlight the natural colors of the cave formations. (And yes, there is a backup lighting system in case of a power outage.)

During the summer at Carlsbad Caverns, the main portion of the cave stays a comfortable fifty-six degrees Fahrenheit, regardless of how hot or humid it gets outside. However, in winter months the temperature of the entire hike down from the entrance to the Big Room can drop to as low as thirty degrees Fahrenheit.

As you continue down through a section called the Devil's Den, imagine how it must have been descending into the depths without the nicely contoured pathway. That's how many park visitors experienced the caverns in the early 1900s.

After about a mile of walking back and forth on the endless series of switchbacks, you come across the famous Iceberg Rock. This gigantic rock (weighing an estimated 200,000 tons!) fell from the ceiling. This was a "big bang" that nobody heard.

Shortly after Iceberg Rock you reach a junction where you can go left to the Underground Lunchroom, elevators, and restrooms or you can continue on and take the Big Room route.

You've now had your mile-long descent into Carlsbad Cavern. You can call it a day and take the elevator to the surface, but if you do, you'll miss the best part of a trip to Carlsbad Cavern, the Big Room.

9 The Big Room

Highlights: A self-guided tour on a paved path.
Start: Visitor center.
Distance: 1.2 miles out and back.
Difficulty: Easy.
Schedule: Any time between 8:30 A.M. and 3:30 P.M. daily May through August and 8:30 A.M. to 2:00 P.M. September through April. No

reservations required. Buy tickets at the visitor center.
Special regulations: No strollers. Stay on cave trails at all times.
Trail contact: Carlsbad Caverns National Park, 3225 National Park Highway, Carlsbad, NM 88220; (505) 785-2232; www.nps.gov/cave.

Finding the trailhead: To find the trailhead, turn west off U.S. Highway 62/180 at Whites City (20 miles south of Carlsbad, New Mexico) and drive 7 miles on a paved road to the park headquarters and visitor center.

The Hike

The Big Room route is the easiest way to see the wonders of Carlsbad Caverns. Since you take the elevator down to the Underground Lunchroom, where the trip starts and ends, the mile-long walk is largely level all the way. You can also extend the Natural Entrance route through the Big Room. A portion of the Big Room route is accessible to visitors using wheelchairs.

The nicely paved route is also lined with superb interpretive displays. And rangers occasionally walk through the cave and will answer questions.

They don't call it the Big Room for nothing. Many of the eighty-two known caves in Carlsbad Caverns National Park have large chambers, but the Big Room is the biggest of them all. The 8.2-acre chamber could encompass six football fields, and the ceiling is 255 feet high. This is the home of the giant speleothems, especially those found in the Hall of Giants, where you can find a 62-foot stalagmite called Giant Dome.

The Big Room also contains the small, elegant formations that complement the huge pillars, making the Big Room a must-see experience. The awe-inspiring expansiveness of the Big Room contains an incredible diversity of cave formations that reflect the fragile and timeless beauty of caves.

10 King's Palace

Highlights: A ranger-guided tour on a paved path.
Start: The Underground Lunchroom, a short elevator ride from the visitor center.
Distance: 0.75 mile out and back.
Difficulty: Moderate.
Schedule: Varies depending on the time of year. Reservations required: call (800) 967-2283.
Special regulations: No strollers. Stay on cave trails at all times.
Trail contact: Carlsbad Caverns National Park, 3225 National Park Highway, Carlsbad, NM 88220; (505) 785-2232; www.nps.gov/cave.

Finding the trailhead: To find the trailhead, turn west off U.S. Highway 62/180 at Whites City (20 miles south of Carlsbad, New Mexico) and drive 7 miles on a paved road to the park headquarters and visitor center.

The Hike

The King's Palace route used to be part of the Natural Entrance self-guided route. However, irresponsible visitors damaged some irreplaceable formations along the route. To prevent further damage, the NPS turned the King's Palace trip into a ranger-guided tour in 1992.

The trip starts in the Underground Lunchroom, where the ranger spends a few minutes summarizing the tour and preparing visitors for the trip. Then the ranger leads you down a paved path to new depths.

The King's Palace route goes through the "scenic rooms" such as the King's Palace, the Queen's Chamber, and the Papoose Room. The scenic rooms have many fantastic cave features, all nicely interpreted by the ranger guiding the trip.

You switchback 80 feet down on a paved trail until you reach a gorgeous cave pool called Green Lake. At this point you're 830 feet below the surface, the deepest point of this trip. That's the equivalent of an eighty-three-story building.

Beyond Green Lake you gradually climb back up to the level of the Underground Lunchroom where the route ends.

11 Lefthand Tunnel

Highlights: An off-trail ranger-guided tour.
Start: The Underground Lunchroom, a short elevator ride from the visitor center.
Distance: 0.5 mile out and back.
Difficulty: Easy.
Schedule: 9:00 A.M. daily. Call (800) 967-2283 for reservations.

Special regulations: Be sure you have good hiking boots or sturdy walking shoes. Stay on cave trails at all times. Limited to fifteen people. No children six or younger.
Trail contact: Carlsbad Caverns National Park, 3225 National Park Highway, Carlsbad, NM 88220; (505) 785-2232; www.nps.gov/cave.

Finding the trailhead: To find the trailhead, turn west off U.S. Highway 62/180 at Whites City (20 miles south of Carlsbad, New Mexico) and drive 7 miles on a paved road to the park headquarters and visitor center.

The Hike

The Lefthand Tunnel trip adds another perspective to the caving experience. It's an off-trail trip, but it's easier than Lower Cave and a walk in the park compared to Spider Cave and Hall of the White Giant. On these wilder routes you're crawling around in the dirt and mud with a headlamp on your hard hat. On the Lefthand Tunnel route, you use a designated path where you can walk upright the entire way with only lanterns for light.

You start the trip right in the Underground Lunchroom. At the far end you go through a rustic old door that immediately sets the historic theme of the trip. You travel through a moderately large tunnel lit only by the dim light of candle lanterns similar to those used by early explorers.

The pale light of the lantern immediately starts you thinking of what it must have been like for the first explorers who braved the depths of Carlsbad Caverns without modern lights or knowledgeable rangers guiding the way. At the turn-around point the rangers have a blackout, where everybody remains totally quiet with only the sounds of the caves permeating the utter blackness. The rangers also tell stories of the early explorations of Carlsbad Caverns.

The trip has some crystal-clear cave pools and lots of examples of fossils in the rocks along the way. It lacks the awe-inspiring formations of other cave routes, but the trip has a special quality of getting you in the right frame of mind. You leave Lefthand Tunnel feeling quite fortunate to have modern conveniences and the National Park Service to take care of you and Carlsbad Caverns.

12 Slaughter Canyon Cave

Highlights: A ranger-guided tour on an undeveloped trail in the cave, plus a short, steep (500-foot elevation gain) hike to the cave entrance.

Start: Slaughter Canyon trailhead.

Distance: 1.25 miles out and back in the cave, plus 0.5 mile each way to reach the cave entrance.

Difficulty: Moderate.

Schedule: Twice daily (10:00 A.M. and 2:00 P.M.) May through August, but only on Saturday and Sunday during winter months. Reservations required: call (800) 967-2283.

Special regulations: No children under age six. Must have bright flashlight with fresh batteries and good walking shoes. Photography permitted, but no tripods. Stay on cave trails at all times. Limited to twenty-five people.

Trail contact: Carlsbad Caverns National Park, 3225 National Park Highway, Carlsbad, NM 88220; (505) 785-2232; www.nps.gov/cave.

Finding the trailhead: To find the trailhead, turn off U.S. Highway 62/180, 6 miles south of Whites City, onto a well-marked paved road, County Road 418. The signs at the turnoff say SLAUGHTER CANYON CAVE and WASHINGTON RANCH. Follow CR 418 for 10 miles until you reach the park boundary and the road turns to gravel. Follow the gravel road for another mile until it dead-ends at the trailhead. There is plenty of parking at the trailhead, which also has toilet and picnic facilities (no toilet facilities beyond this point).

The Hike

Slaughter Canyon Cave is referred to as New Cave by many locals and in some old maps and guidebooks. However, the National Park Service has officially changed the name to Slaughter Canyon Cave. The canyon is named after Charles Slaughter, who ranched here in the early 1900s.

The trail to the cave entrance is the first part of the experience. It's a well-used, well-constructed, well-defined trail—but it's steep! You climb more than 500 feet in a half mile. Since the trip actually starts at the cave entrance (not the trailhead in the parking lot), be sure to leave enough time to climb the hill to the cave so the ranger doesn't leave without you. The door to Slaughter Canyon Cave is always locked, so if you're late, you're out of luck.

This trip is not nearly as wild as others offered by the NPS. You can walk upright the entire way. It's a fairly easy trip with the exception of several slippery spots where the trail goes over ancient flowstone or polished bat guano. Without good-gripping shoes you'll have a tough time in these sections.

Actually, you could call this "the guano walk." For most of the trip, you're walking on bat guano. There's no way to do the trip without stepping in it. Steps have been carved out in many places, but footing is still occasionally difficult.

Fortunately, the guano is about a half-million years old, deposited by an extinct species of bat. It's reddish guano that has had all the nutrients leached out through the centuries. When discovered, there were no bats using the cave, and even now, no

Slaughter Canyon Cave.

bats inhabit the cave, so there is no fresh guano. Miners took 50,000 tons of guano out of the cave, but all five companies that mined the cave went bankrupt because the nutrient-free guano made lousy fertilizer.

Like the Natural Entrance to Carlsbad Caverns, Slaughter Canyon Cave has a great "twilight zone," a short section where the natural light fades into total blackness.

Slaughter Canyon Cave has formations to equal anything in Carlsbad Caverns, such as the Pillars of Hercules (just after the twilight zone), Famous Clansman (filmed as part of the movie *King Solomon's Mines*), and the fabulous Christmas Tree Room. These are definitely among the most spectacular cave formations found anywhere.

Rangers talk frequently about how early miners destroyed parts of the cave before the NPS purchased it from them. At one spot in the cave, you view a pile of trash left by the miners. This spot now has the dubious distinction of being a federally protected junk pile, which is officially called the Slaughter Canyon Cave Museum. It's a good opportunity for the ranger to talk about the lasting impact visitors can have on a cave. Down here, unlike on the surface, there aren't natural processes (wind, water, or sunlight) to wash the impact away.

13 Lower Cave

Highlights: An off-trail ranger-guided tour, a good option for beginning cavers.
Start: Visitor center.
Distance: 1.0 mile out and back.
Difficulty: Moderate.
Schedule: 1:00 P.M. on weekdays. Call (800) 967-2283 for reservations.

Special regulations: Bring your own batteries (four AA alkaline) and be sure you have good hiking boots or sturdy walking shoes. Stay on cave trails at all times. Limited to twelve people. No children under twelve.
Trail contact: Carlsbad Caverns National Park, 3225 National Park Highway, Carlsbad, NM 88220; (505) 785-2232; www.nps.gov/cave.

Finding the trailhead: To find the trailhead, turn west off U.S. Highway 62/180 at Whites City (20 miles south of Carlsbad, New Mexico) and drive 7 miles on a paved road to the park headquarters and visitor center.

The Hike

The trip starts with a meeting at the top of the elevator in the visitor center. Ask at the front desk for directions. The National Park Service often bills the route as a good choice for beginning cavers because you end up doing many things that cavers do, but in an easy form, such as using a hand line, climbing ladders, walking over uneven ground, carefully traversing narrow, decorated passages, and even crawling for a short distance.

After a brief orientation talk by the ranger and an equipment check, you head down the elevator to the Big Room. You take the Big Room route for a short way before turning off and climbing down a series of ladders. In this section the going is difficult and slippery, as you descend 40 feet to Lower Cave.

National Geographic magazine featured the seldom-visited Lower Cave in the early 1900s. Lower Cave has lots of side passages, and several research projects are under way in this, the deepest, section of Carlsbad Caverns.

After the series of ladders, the route is fairly level. However, the trail is undeveloped. There's no nicely contoured, paved path like the Natural Entrance, Big Room, or King's Palace routes. You can walk normally almost all the way, so it also differs from the down-and-dirty Spider Cave and Hall of the White Giant routes.

Perhaps the highlight of the Lower Cave route is the Rookery. Here the ranger points out "nests" of "cave pearls." The Rookery used to be carpeted with cave pearls, but there aren't many left. Apparently, early cave visitors took most of them home for souvenirs. When you get to the Jumping Off Point, the ceiling is high enough to clear a twelve-story building with a few feet to spare.

The Lower Cave route is a nice option for visitors who want more than the self-guided tours but aren't ready to be amateur cavers.

14 Spider Cave

Highlights: An off-trail ranger-guided adventure tour.
Start: Visitor center.
Distance: About 1 mile out and back, plus 0.5 mile each way to and from the cave entrance.
Difficulty: Difficult.
Schedule: 1:00 P.M. on Sunday only. Call (800) 967-2283 for reservations.

Special regulations: Bring four AA alkaline batteries. Be sure you have good hiking boots or sturdy walking shoes, gloves, and long pants. Limited to eight people. No children under twelve. Old clothes are strongly recommended, as you're going to get dirty on this trip.
Trail contact: Carlsbad Caverns National Park, 3225 National Park Highway, Carlsbad, NM 88220; (505) 785-2232; www.nps.gov/cave.

Finding the trailhead: To find the trailhead, turn west off U.S. Highway 62/180 at Whites City (20 miles south of Carlsbad, New Mexico) and drive 7 miles on a paved road to the park headquarters and visitor center.

The Hike

At the visitor center the rangers equip you with lights and knee and elbow pads and give a short orientation talk. Then the group drives their own vehicles about 1 mile to the parking area at the beginning of Scenic Loop Drive. From the parking area you hike about 0.5 mile into nearby Garden Grove Canyon, down a steep descent to the dry wash and the entrance to Spider Cave. This is a difficult, but short, hike.

Experienced cavers love Spider Cave, but it can be intimidating for the novice. Even the name is intimidating, and yes, the cave was named for the hordes of "spiders" clinging to the ceiling when it was discovered, but they're gone now. Technically, the cave was misnamed. In reality it should be called Harvestmen Cave. The "spiders" the early explorers found were actually harvestmen (i.e., daddy longlegs), which are arachnids but technically not spiders.

Then, after you get past the arachnophobia, it gets worse. The entrance to the cave has been built up out of the arroyo like the opening to a manhole. As the ranger unlocks the "manhole cover," it's easy to wonder what the National Park Service has locked up down there.

You then climb down a ladder and crawl through a narrow, muddy passage for 50 yards or so. Hopefully, your arachnophobia doesn't turn to claustrophobia, because you can't go back. It's too tight to turn around.

The group stops for a rest in the first big chamber. This doesn't happen on the guided tour, but if the ranger decided to have the blackout early and be really quiet at this point, inexperienced cavers might hear the real sounds of a narrow cave passage—adrenaline flowing and hearts pounding.

Although the initial rush might test your courage, the trip soon turns into a fantastic experience. You're not likely to forget your trip to Spider Cave. In fact, if the

NPS wanted to convert park visitors into cavers, the trip to Spider Cave would be a great introduction.

If you've already been in the Big Room, you'll notice the stark contrast with Spider Cave. Everything seems to be miniature in comparison—some of the same type of speleothems, but they are 6 feet instead of 60 feet tall, and equally beautiful. Most of the rock and dirt in Spider Cave is a reddish color, which contrasts sharply with many splendid white formations.

Spider Cave has about 3 miles of explored passages, but this trip is less than a mile long. Even though the cave is near Carlsbad Caverns, there is no known connection.

On this trip, like many others, rangers spend time discussing cave preservation by showing how early explorers destroyed precious formations. Once despoiled, cave features are extremely difficult or impossible to reclaim and, of course, it would take several million years to grow them again.

This is an underground wilderness, a place for truly getting away from it all and being awed by the wonders and curiosities of nature. It's also a chance to do something relatively few others have done and see things few others have seen.

15 Hall of the White Giant

Highlights: An off-trail ranger-guided tour.
Start: Visitor center.
Distance: 0.5 mile out and back.
Difficulty: Difficult.
Schedule: 1:00 P.M. on Saturday only. Call (800) 967-2283 for reservations.
Special regulations: Bring four AA alkaline batteries. Be sure you have good hiking boots or sturdy walking shoes, gloves, and long pants. Limited to eight people. No children under twelve.
Trail contact: Carlsbad Caverns National Park, 3225 National Park Highway, Carlsbad, NM 88220; (505) 785-2232; www.nps.gov/cave.

Finding the trailhead: To find the trailhead, turn west off U.S. Highway 62/180 at Whites City (20 miles south of Carlsbad, New Mexico) and drive 7 miles on a paved road to the park headquarters and visitor center.

The Hike

This trip, like Spider Cave, adds a whole new dimension to a visit to Carlsbad Caverns. This is one of the "wild caving experiences" the National Park Service mentions in its literature.

After getting equipped with hard hats, headlamps, and knee and elbow pads and hearing a brief introduction by the ranger, you head out of the visitor center on the Natural Entrance route. About halfway down the ranger stops and directs you to a small passage, which—compared to the huge cavern you're standing in—doesn't

Signing the register at the end of the trip to the Hall of the White Giant.

even look like a cave. In fact, if you walked down the manicured path from the Natural Entrance on an earlier trip, you obviously walked right past the entrance to the passage leading to the Hall of the White Giant without even noticing it.

It's only a half mile, but it takes more than three hours. Along the way you'll use (or quickly learn) some beginning rock-climbing skills like chimneying. You also climb up and down well-placed ladders, over slippery flowstone, and through some incredibly tight spots to reach your goal—the Hall of the White Giant.

The White Giant might not be as spectacular as the giant formations in the Big Room, King's Palace, or Slaughter Canyon Cave, but all the work you have to do to see it might make the White Giant the most spectacular of them all. When you get there, you'll take turns using a rope to climb over slick flowstone to get a closer view of the magnificent formation. Then, after everybody has had a turn, the ranger does the traditional blackout to give you the stark essence of the cave.

Guadalupe Mountains National Park

N amed after the patron saint of Mexico, the Guadalupe Mountains highlight the horizon of west Texas. The mountain range contains the four tallest peaks in Texas and what has frequently been called "the best view in Texas," the vista from the top of Hunter Peak. Another section of the park, McKittrick Canyon, has been labeled "the most beautiful spot in Texas."

In these mountains, which loom 3,700 feet above the salt flats of northwestern Texas, the plants and animals of the desert meet those of the mountains, and the southern species meet the northern species. They all make a home, together and symbolically, here in the Guadalupes.

The 86,416-acre park provides a fragile environment for 58 mammal, 260 bird, and hundreds of distinct plant species. "The National Park Highway" (U.S. Highway 62/180) provides tantalizing glimpses of the beauty beyond, especially the protruding landmark El Capitan, visible for 50 miles in any direction. Three major trailheads provide access to the backcountry, and more than 80 miles of trails offer scenic avenues for the human species to see it all.

The Pine Springs trailhead leads to most of the park's trails, and it has a campground, picnic area, and visitor center (open 8:00 A.M. to 6:00 P.M. during daylight savings time and 8:00 A.M. to 4:30 P.M. the rest of the year). McKittrick Canyon trailhead offers an easy and popular trail through the incredible beauty and diversity of that hidden canyon. But at an elevation of 6,300 feet, the secluded Dog Canyon trailhead offers the easiest route to the heart of the Guadalupes.

Guadalupe Mountains National Park is a haven for both geologists and botanists. Even visitors totally unfamiliar with and uninterested in geology and botany routinely leave the park as amateur botanists and geologists.

Entrance sign with El Capitan in the background. NPS PHOTO BY D. ALLEN.

The trail system is very well constructed, maintained, and organized. The National Park Service has worked hard to provide great trails, and the extra effort really shows. The trail system offers the variety and convenience many hikers prefer. This book outlines the most popular routes, but the trail system allows the creative hiker to craft his or her own adventures. Only the Blue Ridge Trail and Marcus Trail in the far northwestern corner of the park are less-than-ideal trails.

To fully enjoy the Guadalupes, however, hikers must be in a proper frame of mind.

First, get water out of your mind. The Guadalupes have no reliable water sources. Although your pack can grow heavy with the weight of water, you'll soon realize that a landscape does not need a mountain lake or waterfall to be scenic.

Second, the wind can really blow, especially in the spring. And this isn't a wimpy wind like you find in Chicago. This is a real, herculean wind, often gusting to more than 50 mph and as fast as 125 mph. It's weird, too. It comes up suddenly, blows you off the trail, and then goes away, only to return when you least expect it. You can be walking along, leaning into the wind at a forty-five-degree angle, and then, just like that, it stops blowing and you fall down. Instead of looking at the wind as a problem, look at it as a special feature and challenge of the Guadalupes.

You can hike year-round in the Guadalupes, but the summer heat can be miserable, and snow can blanket the high country during winter months. The "shoulder seasons"—March through May and September through November—usually offer the best hiking weather.

Getting to Guadalupe Mountains National Park

From El Paso, Texas, drive east 110 miles on US 62/180 to Pine Springs, the location of the park headquarters and visitor center. From Carlsbad, New Mexico, drive south 56 miles on US 62/180 into Texas to Pine Springs. If you're flying in and renting a car, it's best to use the El Paso airport. Keep in mind that there are no services within 30 miles of the park, so arrive there with a full tank of gas and all the supplies you need for your stay.

Pine Springs Trailhead

The Pine Springs area serves as the park headquarters. It has a large visitor center, the park's largest campground, and a sizable picnic area. The trailhead is located at the far end of the campground. There's plenty of parking, and hikers can get backcountry camping permits at the nearby visitor center.

This is a major trailhead. Trails go in all directions, and in fact, the majority of the park's trails can be reached from here.

The Pine Springs area also has a rich and colorful history. The Butterfield Stage Route passed through here; the ruins of a stagecoach station, the Pinery, lie near the visitor center. The U.S. Army used the area before the Civil War and after the campaign against the Mescalero Apache.

The main reason for all the early activity was a reliable water source at Lower Pine Springs. However, the spring dried up after a 1931 earthquake.

Finding the Trailhead

Turn off of US 62/180 at the main entrance of Guadalupe Mountains National Park. Immediately take a left turn into the campground. Drive to the far end of the campground to the well-marked trailhead. The trailhead has toilet facilities and a large parking lot. If the lot is full, you can also park in the visitor center parking lot and use a short connecting trail to get from the visitor center to the trailhead. Don't park in the marked campsites in the nearby campground.

Also included in the Pine Springs Trailhead section of this book are trails leaving the Williams Ranch and the Frijole Ranch. Please refer to these trails for specific directions to these trailheads.

16 The Pinery

Highlights: A self-guided interpretive trail.
Start: Pine Springs Visitor Center, or a turnoff from U.S. Highway 62/180 just 1 mile north of the park headquarters.
Distance: 0.75-mile loop.
Difficulty: Easy; accessible to people with mobility impairments.

Maps: Free park brochure available at visitor center.
Trail contact: Guadalupe Mountains National Park, H.C. 60, Box 400, Salt Flat, TX 79847-9400; (915) 828-3251; www.nps.gov/gamo.

The Hike

For a brief introduction to the low-elevation environment of Guadalupe Mountains National Park, take this short nature trail from the visitor center to the Pinery. The trail starts right at the front door of the Pine Springs Visitor Center.

The trail gets its name from an old stagecoach horse-changing station located on the Butterfield Trail, a 2,800-mile overland mail route used in the 1800s. The station, located on 5,534-foot Guadalupe Pass, was named for the stands of pine nearby. Today, US 62/180 generally follows the stage route through Guadalupe Pass.

The Pinery Trail is a paved, self-guided tour with excellent interpretive signs covering the history of the area and offering tantalizing details on several plant species in the area. You travel about 0.25 mile from the visitor center to the ruins of the station, then around the ruins and back to the visitor center. You can also have somebody pick you up at the parking lot on US 62/180 just north of the turnoff to Pine Springs.

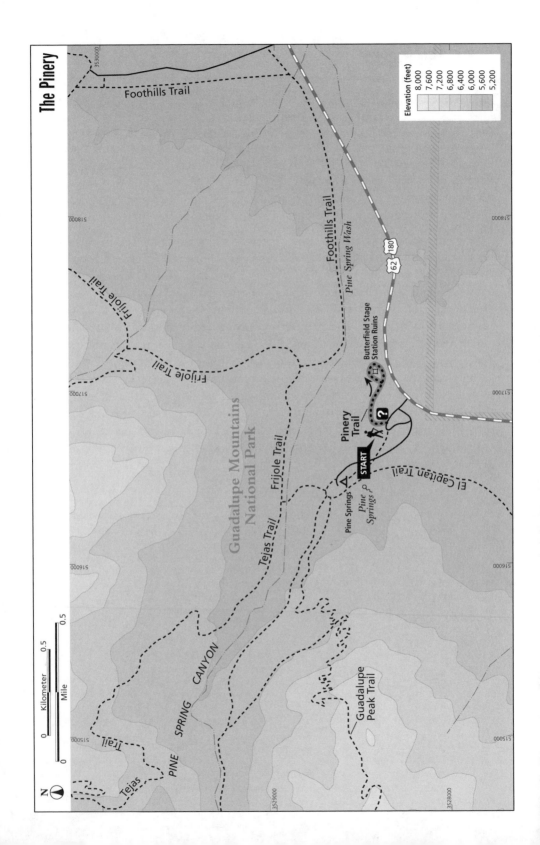

The Pinery

N

Kilometer
0   0.5

Mile
0   0.5

Foothills Trail

Foothills Trail

Frijole Trail

Frijole Trail

Pine Spring Wash

Butterfield Stage
Station Ruins

62 180

Pinery
Trail

?

START

El Capitan Trail

Pine Springs

Pine Springs

Frijole Trail

Tejas Trail

Guadalupe Mountains
National Park

Guadalupe
Peak Trail

PINE SPRING CANYON

Tejas Trail

Elevation (feet)
8,000
7,600
7,200
6,800
6,400
6,000
5,600
5,200

17 Salt Basin Overlook

Highlights: A moderately long day hike with memorable scenery.
Start: Pine Springs trailhead.
Distance: 11.5-mile lollipop loop.
Difficulty: Moderate.

Maps: Trails Illustrated: Guadalupe Mountains; USGS: Guadalupe Peak and Guadalupe Pass; park brochure.
Trail contact: Guadalupe Mountains National Park, H.C. 60, Box 400, Salt Flat, TX 79847-9400; (915) 828–3251; www.nps.gov/gamo.

The Hike

For those who want a long day hike without much climbing, the Salt Basin Overlook Trail is an excellent choice. Set aside a entire day for this trip, which leaves an hour or two for relaxing along the way. The trail is well defined all the way with the exception of one short stretch where it dips into Guadalupe Canyon on the lower loop.

About 100 feet after leaving the campground, the trail forks and then forks again in another 100 feet. Take the left fork at both junctions.

The trail climbs gradually (460 feet in about 3 miles) toward El Capitan before dropping into beautiful Guadalupe Canyon, where you'll find the junction with the Salt Basin Overlook Trail. You'll start getting good looks at El Capitan after about 1.5 miles. If you're taking the loop, it's easier to continue on straight (southwest) on the El Capitan Trail for 0.9 mile to the second junction, and then take the loop counterclockwise.

The views from the El Capitan Trail equal those from any place on the loop, so if you're interested in an 8.6-mile hike instead of an 11.5-mile hike, you can make this an out-and-back hike by retracing your steps back to the campground from the second junction and call it a good day. The loop adds 3.6 miles of new terrain to the trip, but from a scenery standpoint it doesn't add much.

If you take the loop, the trail drops sharply from the second junction (a good reason to do the loop counterclockwise) down to the ruins of an old water tank. Along this half-mile stretch you get great views into the salt flats to the southwest. Be sure to look back a few times to view the stately El Capitan looming over you to the north. At about the 3-mile mark on the loop, the trail drops down into an arroyo for about 0.25 mile, but cairns lead the way.

The wind often whips through this area, especially in the spring and especially around the second junction, so hang on to your hat. Just when it starts to seem like you've been trapped in a hair drier for life, the wind suddenly stops blowing.

Also, there is virtually no shade along this route, so be prepared for a full day in the sun.

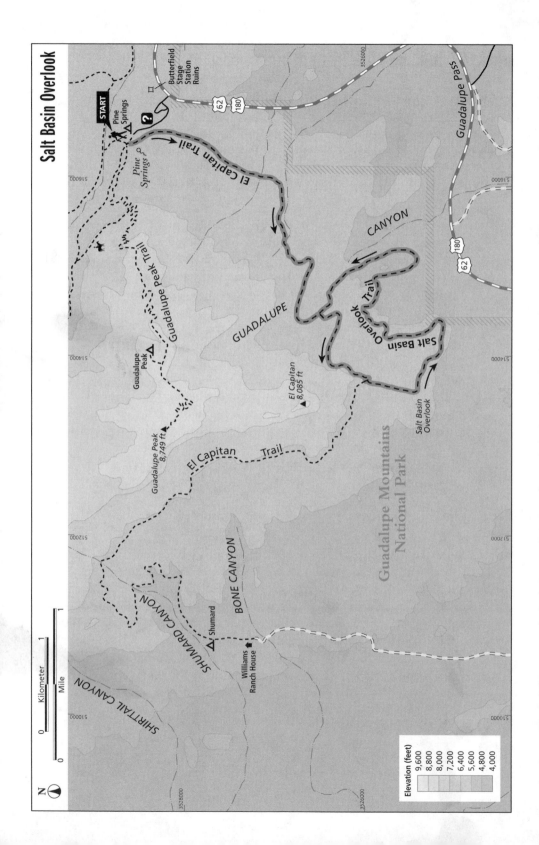

Salt Basin Overlook

START

Pine Springs

Butterfield Stage Station Ruins

62 180

Guadalupe Pass

Pine Springs

El Capitan Trail

GUADALUPE

CANYON

Guadalupe Peak Trail

Guadalupe Peak

Salt Basin Overlook Trail

62 180

El Capitan 8,085 ft

Guadalupe Peak 8,749 ft

Salt Basin Overlook

El Capitan Trail

Guadalupe Mountains National Park

SHIRTTAIL CANYON

SHUMARD CANYON

BONE CANYON

Shumard

Williams Ranch House

N

Kilometer

Mile

0   1

Elevation (feet)
9,600
8,800
8,000
7,200
6,400
5,600
4,800
4,000

516000
516000
514000
514000
512000
512000
510000
510000

3528000
3526000
3526000

Miles and Directions

0.0 Start at the Pine Springs trailhead and follow the El Capitan Trail.

3.4 In Guadalupe Canyon, turn right at the junction with the Salt Basin Overlook loop trail.

4.3 At the second junction with the loop trail, turn left.

7.9 At the junction with the main trail at Guadalupe Canyon (El Capitan Trail), turn right.

11.5 Reach the Pine Springs trailhead.

18 El Capitan

Highlights: A long day hike in a more remote section of the park.
Start: Williams Ranch.
Distance: 9.4-mile shuttle.
Difficulty: Moderate.

Maps: Trails Illustrated: Guadalupe Mountains; USGS: PX Flat and Guadalupe Peak; park brochure.
Trail contact: Guadalupe Mountains National Park, H.C. 60, Box 400, Salt Flat, TX 79847-9400; (915) 828-3251; www.nps.gov/gamo.

Finding the trailhead: The first step in getting to the trailhead is a visit to the visitor center, where you ask for a key to the gates on the way to the Williams Ranch. This is a four-wheel-drive road—definitely not for low-clearance vehicles. Park regulations prohibit leaving vehicles at the trailhead, so you must arrange for someone to drop you off.

To find the trailhead, drive south on U.S. Highway 62/180 from the main entrance to Guadalupe Mountains National Park for 8 miles and turn right (west). Be alert, as this turn is poorly marked, with no sign except a National Park Service shield on the brown gate. Use the key to unlock the gate and then be sure to lock it behind you, and ditto for a second gate about a mile up the road. The NPS has arranged public access across this mile-long strip of private land paralleling the highway, but remember this is private land, so be sure to stay on the road.

Beyond the second gate you're in the park. Slowly bump and grind up the road, which gets rough in places, until it ends at the Williams Ranch trailhead. It takes about an hour to get to Williams Ranch from the visitor center.

The Hike

This is definitely one of the most spectacular hikes in the Guadalupe Mountains. Unfortunately, it requires some special effort to arrange a shuttle to Williams Ranch. When you get out on the trail, however, you'll consider the extra hassle worth it compared to the effort involved in making this an 18.8-mile, out-and-back hike from Pine Springs.

You could consider getting to the trailhead as part of the experience. The primitive road to the trailhead generally follows parts of the Butterfield Stage Route used in the mid-1800s. In the early 1900s the Williams Ranch was a working ranching operation where Robert Belcher ran longhorn cattle. Later, Uncle Dolph Williams

Williams Ranch at the Shumard Canyon trailhead.

ran cattle, sheep, and goats there until 1942. The NPS has preserved the historic ranch house at the trailhead. On the way to Williams Ranch, you can see the aftermath of overgrazing in this dry climate, as the original grassland has been replaced by an ocean of creosote.

This is the only trail into the remote western portion of the Guadalupe Mountains. Don't plan on seeing many people (at least until you get to the Guadalupe Canyon area), because this area receives much less use than most other trails in the park. Starting from the west end at Williams Ranch allows you to end at the Pine Springs campground and have the often strong westerly winds at your back most of the way.

From the trailhead the trail climbs up Shumard Canyon. The grade doesn't seem steep, but it's a healthy climb, gaining over 1,300 feet in the first 2 miles. The scenery is spectacular, which may be one reason the climb doesn't seem as precipitous as it is. At several points while climbing up the canyon, you get great views down the canyon and out into the flats to the west. Ahead you can see Shumard Peak and the great escarpment of the Guadalupe Mountains.

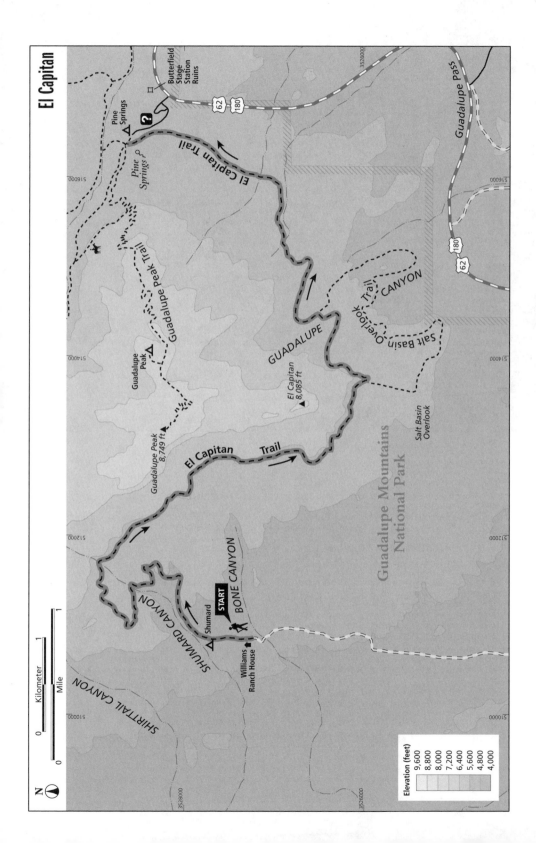

El Capitan

N

Elevation (feet)
9,600
8,800
8,000
7,200
6,400
5,600
4,800
4,000

Kilometer
0   1
Mile
0   1

SHIRTTAIL CANYON

SHUMARD CANYON

Williams Ranch House

Shumard

START

BONE CANYON

El Capitan   Trail

Guadalupe Peak
8,749 ft

Guadalupe Peak

Guadalupe Peak Trail

El Capitan
8,085 ft

GUADALUPE

CANYON

Salt Basin Overlook Trail

Salt Basin Overlook

Pine Springs

Pine Springs

El Capitan Trail

Butterfield Stage Station Ruins

62 180

Guadalupe Mountains National Park

Guadalupe Pass

62 180

The trail up Shumard Canyon.

About 0.4 mile from the trailhead, you'll find the designated Shumard campsite, for backpackers only. It's well signed and about 100 yards off to the left (west), with five tent sites all flattened and rock-free, thanks to the NPS.

Beyond the head of Shumard Canyon, the trail turns south, levels out, and passes the head of sprawling Bone Canyon. For the next 3 miles, you hike in the shadow of the Guadalupe escarpment, gradually gaining another 200 feet. You essentially walk around El Capitan, the venerable symbol of Guadalupe Mountains National Park. You can look down and see the cars traveling the highway below, but you have a much better view than these travelers do.

After 5.1 miles you reach the first junction with the Salt Basin Overlook Trail. If you want to stretch the hike out for an additional 3.6 miles, take the lower loop trail. However, this lower loop adds little more than distance to the trip. The scenery from above at least equals anything you see on the lower loop.

After another 0.9 mile you drop down into Guadalupe Canyon, where you find the other end of the lower loop trail. From here it's 3.4 miles to the Pine Springs trailhead, all fairly level and easy walking.

The El Capitan Trail is better suited for a long day hike than an overnighter. The Shumard campsite is located at the beginning (or the end) of the trail, which means you must hike the entire trail in one day whether you do an overnighter or a day hike. However, for the well-conditioned hiker this can be a nice overnight, out-and-back trip from the Pine Springs trailhead if you don't have somebody to give you a ride around to the Williams Ranch.

This trail is well defined and easy to follow the entire way. Just before you reach the Pine Springs trailhead, the trail forks twice. Take the right fork at both junctions.

Miles and Directions

0.0   Start at the Williams Ranch trailhead.

0.4   Pass the Shumard campsite on the left.

4.6   Reach El Capitan.

5.1   At the first junction with the lower loop trail, turn left.

6.0   At the second junction with the lower loop trail, turn left.

9.4   Reach the Pine Springs trailhead.

19 Guadalupe Peak

Highlights: The marquee hike in the park, a must-see trip to the highest point in Texas.
Start: Pine Springs trailhead.
Distance: 8.4 miles out and back.
Difficulty: Difficult.

Maps: Trails Illustrated: Guadalupe Mountains; USGS: Guadalupe Peak; park brochure.
Trail contact: Guadalupe Mountains National Park, H.C. 60, Box 400, Salt Flat, TX 79847-9400; (915) 828-3251; www.nps.gov/gamo.

The Hike

For more than one reason, this trail is the high point of Guadalupe Mountains National Park. Guadalupe Peak is the highest spot not only in the park but also in all of Texas. At 8,749 feet Guadalupe Peak might pale in comparison to the 14,000-foot summits of California and Colorado, but in terms of relief, elevation gain, and sheer beauty, it can be compared with any mountain in the lower forty-eight states.

Besides taking you to the highest elevation in the park, the trip to Guadalupe Peak is bound to be the "high point" of any visit to the park. In fact, this is one of the most spectacular hikes in the United States. If you only have one day to hike in the Guadalupe Mountains and your fitness level is average or better, this hike should be your top priority.

If possible, start early. This hike climbs nearly 3,000 feet, so you want to take advantage of the cooler temperatures of the early morning. Take plenty of water.

Guadalupe Peak and El Capitan viewed from the ridge above Pine Springs Canyon.

The trail climbs the entire 4.2 miles to the highest point in Texas, but fortunately it has been expertly constructed to minimize the damage to your legs and lungs. Nonetheless, it's a tough hike, so get ready to put out some sweat to reach the summit. This trail will certainly dispel lingering myths about Texas being flat.

The National Park Service allows horses on this trail to within 100 yards of the summit, but horse use is limited, as the serious elevation gain with no water sources makes this trail too difficult for many horses. Backcountry horsemen take the longer route (see map) instead of the steeper 0.7-mile segment reserved for hikers only.

After about 2 miles you might believe you see the top and start thinking you were in better shape than you thought. But beware, this is a false summit; you're only about halfway there. You might want to occupy your mind studying the major shift in biomes—from desert vegetation like cactus and yucca to the higher-elevation pine forests.

A mile before the summit, watch for a sign for the campground, which lies on a rare level spot on the mountain about 200 yards to the right of the main trail. This is the highest campground in Texas, and it's so special that it's probably worth the 2,000-foot climb with a heavy pack to get there. There are five flattened, rock-free

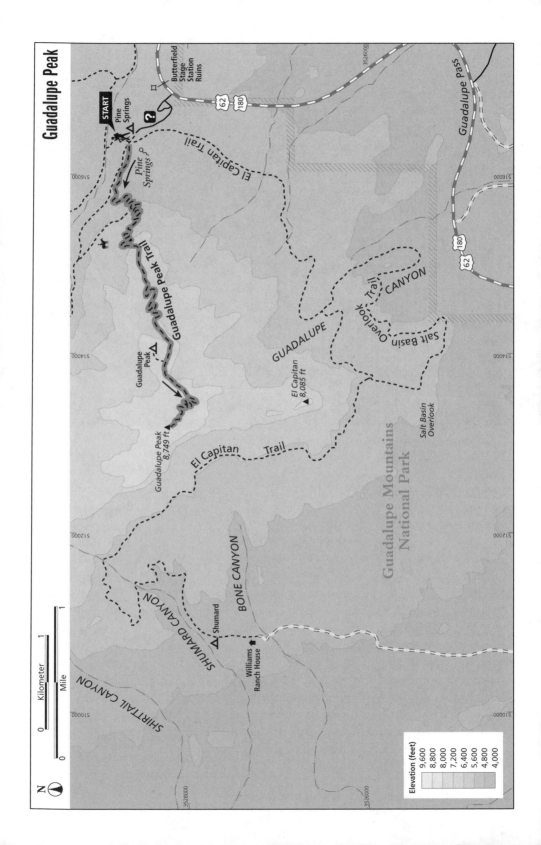

Guadalupe Peak

N

Elevation (feet)
9,600
8,800
8,000
7,200
6,400
5,600
4,800
4,000

Kilometer 1
Mile 1

Guadalupe Mountains National Park

START
Pine Springs

Butterfield Stage Station Ruins

62 180 US

Guadalupe Pass

Pine Springs

El Capitan Trail

Guadalupe Peak Trail

Guadalupe Peak

Guadalupe Peak 8,749 ft

El Capitan Trail

El Capitan 8,085 ft

GUADALUPE

CANYON

Salt Basin Overlook Trail

Salt Basin Overlook

62 180 US

SHIRTTAIL CANYON

SHUMARD CANYON

Shumard

BONE CANYON

Williams Ranch House

3528000
3526000
516000
514000
512000
510000
508000
506000
3522000
3520000

The top of El Capitan from the Guadalupe Peak Trail.

tent sites with spectacular views. It would be hard to beat the amenities of this campground. If you decide to camp overnight, stake your tent well, as the wind can be vicious on Guadalupe Peak, especially in the spring.

At the summit you obviously get the grandest view possible. Bush Mountain (8,631 feet) and Shumard Peak (8,615 feet) to the north are the second- and third-highest peaks in Texas. To the south stretches the vast flatness of the Chihauhuan Desert, broken only by the Delaware and Sierra Diablos Mountains. On a clear day you can see the 12,003-foot Sierra Blanca, more than 100 miles to the north.

After taking in the vistas all around, you might want to write some stirring personal impressions in the trail register at the top. In 1958 American Airlines placed a pyramid-shaped monument on the summit to commemorate the one-hundredth anniversary of transcontinental mail delivery, which went through Guadalupe Pass.

On the way down you can see Pine Springs campground and say "I climbed up here!" You also get a great view of Hunter Peak (8,368 feet) and the massive Pine Springs Canyon. You can also see the Tejas Trail angling up the south side of Hunter Peak.

When you finally reach the campground, you can relax for a while and relish in the thought that you will leave the Guadalupe Mountains with the lifelong memory of a truly unforgettable hike.

Miles and Directions

0.0 Start at the Pine Springs trailhead.

0.1 At the junction with the Guadalupe Peak horse trail, turn left.

0.8 At the second junction with the Guadalupe Peak horse trail, turn left.

3.2 Reach the Guadalupe Peak campground.

4.2 Reach the summit of Guadalupe Peak.

8.4 Return to the Pine Springs trailhead.

20 Devil's Hall

Highlights: A nice day hike to an unusually narrow canyon.
Start: Pine Springs trailhead.
Distance: 4.2 miles out and back.
Difficulty: Moderate.

Maps: Trails Illustrated: Guadalupe Mountains; USGS: Guadalupe Peak; park brochure.
Trail contact: Guadalupe Mountains National Park, H.C. 60, Box 400, Salt Flat, TX 79847-9400; (915) 828-3251; www.nps.gov/gamo.

The Hike

The first mile of this trip follows a well-defined trail up Pine Springs Canyon. This is the horse route up Guadalupe Peak, so the trail is easy to follow.

The trail passes through the scars left by the man-caused, 6,510-acre Pine Fire of 1993. This is a stark reminder to be careful with fire in this dry, fragile environment. Note that this fire, like most wildland fires, did not burn everything. Instead, wildfire tends to leave some plants unburnt, which helps re-vegetate the area.

At the end of the first mile, the main trail switchbacks to the left toward the Guadalupe Peak Trail. At this switchback you'll notice a sign indicating that the trail continues along the canyon wash. Go straight on the less-developed trail.

For the first 100 yards after the sign, the trail is rocky and rough, and then it disappears completely. You spend most of the rest of the trip walking up the canyon wash. It's another mile to Devil's Hall.

The walking gets rough here and there, so pick your way carefully. Watch for small and infrequent cairns, but don't panic if you can't see one. You won't get lost as long as you stay in the streambed.

Just before Devil's Hall the canyon narrows at a spot sometimes called Devil's Gate. Shortly thereafter, you go up a stair-step-like series of ledges called the Hiker's

Devil's Hall. NPS PHOTO BY D. ALLEN.

Staircase. Then you can see where the canyon has been pinched down to about 15 feet at Devil's Hall.

Devil's Hall is an unusual spot where the streambed narrows and slips between two pillars of rock. Much of the rock in the area looks like it was laid down like fine masonry.

Although the rock formations seem to be the focal point of this trip, they might not be the most scenic part of the hike. That distinction might go to the diverse and colorful vegetation in the area. The entire hike goes through the desert riparian zone, but the last mile follows a narrow canyon where the shade provided by the canyon walls and the extra vegetation of the streambed has created a showcase of dryland flora. The canyon is lined with velvet ash, Texas madrone, bigtooth maple, ponderosa pine, and many other tree species. In the fall it can be almost as colorful as McKittrick Canyon, but with fewer people.

For beginning hikers this hike provides an opportunity to gain confidence by getting off trail—and surviving.

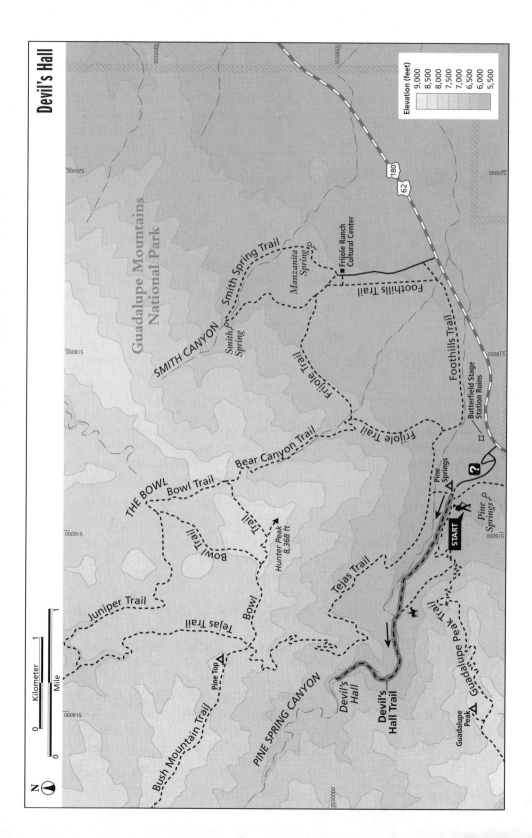

The National Park Service advises against going any farther up the canyon than Devil's Hall, and a sign marks the end of the trail. After taking a good break, retrace your steps to the campground. If you have the time and energy, you can take a different route back, by taking a right when you hit the main trail again and, after 0.6 mile, taking another left down the Guadalupe Peak Trail to the campground.

One note of caution: Avoid this hike on afternoons when thunderstorms are likely. You would not want to be caught at Devil's Hall in a flash flood.

Miles and Directions

0.0 Start at the Pine Springs trailhead.

1.0 At the junction with Devil's Hall Trail, turn right.

2.1 Arrive at Devil's Hall (your turnaround point).

3.2 At the junction with Devil's Hall Trail, turn left. **Option:** Take a right at this junction and, after 0.6 mile, take a left down the Guadalupe Peak Trail back to the trailhead.

4.2 Reach the Pine Springs trailhead.

21 Hunter Peak

Highlights: A terrific loop hike with outstanding high-altitude scenery.
Start: Pine Springs trailhead.
Distance: 8.5-mile loop.
Difficulty: Difficult.

Maps: Trails Illustrated: Guadalupe Mountains; USGS: Guadalupe Peak; park brochure.
Trail contact: Guadalupe Mountains National Park, H.C. 60, Box 400, Salt Flat, TX 79847-9400; (915) 828-3251; www.nps.gov/gamo.

The Hike

When considering this hike, one big question comes up right away—clockwise or counterclockwise? This question is often debated among local hikers and park rangers with, unfortunately, no consensus. It really comes down to personal preference. Do you prefer to gain elevation fast and get it behind you as quickly as possible? Or do you like a long, gradual climb without as many steep grades? Counterclockwise is easier on the knees, but clockwise is easier on the lungs.

If you're in the "get it over with" camp, go counterclockwise, proceeding up Bear Canyon and down the Tejas Trail (3.9 miles to the high point just below Hunter Peak, with most of the elevation gained in a 1.8-mile stretch up Bear Canyon). If you like a longer, more gradual climb, go clockwise, trekking up the Tejas Trail and down Bear Canyon (4.8 miles to the same high point, with a moderate grade most of the way). This trail description is written for the clockwise route.

Immediately after leaving Pine Springs campground, you take a right at a major junction, with trails going off to the left to Guadalupe Peak and El Capitan and

The Butterfield Stage station with Hunter Peak in the background. NPS PHOTO BY F. MANY.

straight to Devil's Hall. You go right on the Frijole Trail. Then, in another 200 yards or so, after crossing the expansive dry wash of Pine Springs Canyon, you hit another junction, with the Frijole Trail going straight. Turn left and head north up the hill on the Tejas Trail. You'll be coming back down the Frijole Trail.

The next mile is nearly flat with an almost imperceptible increase in elevation. Then you start a moderate climb up to Pine Top, about 2,000 vertical feet over 3 miles of well-designed trail that minimizes the impact of the elevation gain. This trail is as good as a trail can be, but it still doesn't make this an easy hike, especially on a hot day with an overnight pack. Plan on two to three hours to get to Pine Top—and longer if you have a heavy pack.

Like many spots in the Guadalupe Mountains, especially in the spring, the wind can whip through Pine Springs Canyon. You can try to forget the wind by watching the vegetation gradually change, switchback after switchback, and then dramatically change the instant you crest the edge of the escarpment and enter the high-altitude forest of ponderosa pine, limber pine, and Douglas fir.

If you're staying overnight, you must have a permit for the Pine Top campground, which is 0.2 mile to your left when you enter the forest. The campground

View of Pine Springs area from the top of Bear Canyon.

has six tent sites all leveled and squared, courtesy of the National Park Service. This campground has a better view than many other campsites in the park. To finish the loop, you'll have to retrace that 0.2 mile the next morning.

If you're day hiking, take a right at the junction at the top of the escarpment (the 4.2-mile mark) and head east on the Bowl Trail toward Hunter Peak. After a long half mile, the Middle Bowl Trail splits, and you take the right-hand fork, staying on the rim of the escarpment.

Shortly after the split you'll see a spur trail heading off to the right and climbing up to 8,368-foot Hunter Peak. This junction is the high point of the main trail, but it's another 150 vertical feet or so to the top of Hunter Peak on the spur trail. If you're backpacking, shed your pack here and take the 0.25-mile climb up to the top of Hunter Peak for a rest break and a great view of Guadalupe Peak and El Capitan and of the entire Pine Springs and Frijole area—plus, it seems, all of Texas. It looks like you're level with Guadalupe Peak, but Hunter Peak is 381 feet lower.

After dropping down to the main trail, you finally start going downhill. In less than a half mile, you'll see the junction with the Bear Canyon Trail. You'll also be

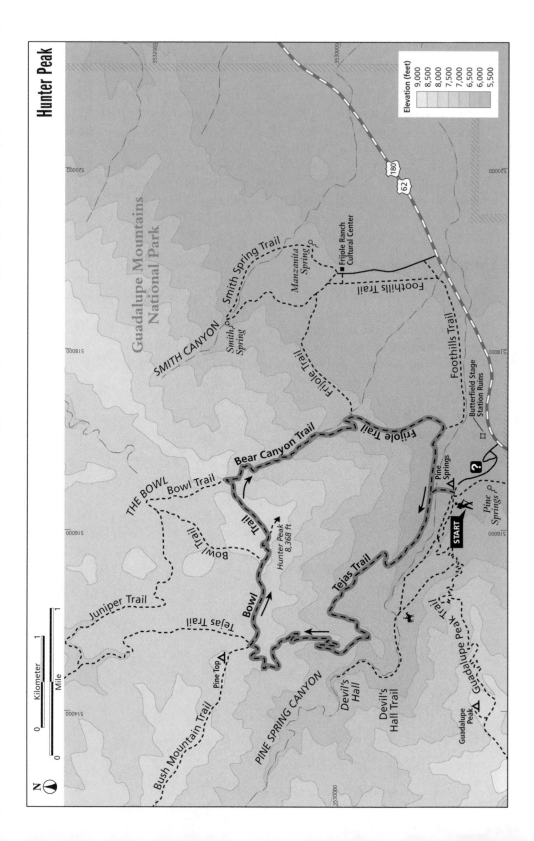

Hunter Peak

N

Guadalupe Mountains
National Park

Elevation (feet)

9,000
8,500
8,000
7,500
7,000
6,500
6,000
5,500

SMITH CANYON

Smith Spring Trail

Smith
Spring

Manzanita
Spring

Frijole Ranch
Cultural Center

Frijole Trail

Frijole Trail

Foothills Trail

Foothills Trail

Butterfield Stage
Station Ruins

180
62

Bear Canyon Trail

THE BOWL

Bowl Trail

Bowl Trail

Hunter Peak
8,368 ft

Bowl Trail

Juniper Trail

Tejas Trail

Bush Mountain Trail

Pine Top

Tejas Trail

PINE SPRING CANYON

Devil's Hall

Devil's
Hall Trail

Guadalupe Peak Trail

Guadalupe
Peak

Pine
Springs

Pine
Springs

START

Kilometer

Mile

3532000
3530000

520000
518000
516000
514000

518000
516000
512000

able to see how steep the narrow canyon is compared with the longer switchbacks up the Tejas Trail. You might also wonder how (and why!) ranchers in the early 1900s pumped water for livestock all the way up Bear Canyon. Some hikers might find this stretch of trail too steep to comfortably hike without slipping or feeling some pain in their knees, but it's short, only 1.8 miles to the junction with the Frijole Trail.

By the time you reach the Frijole Trail, you've seen a rapid change in the vegetation, going from the pine forest, through riparian vegetation like bigtooth maple, and then out into the yucca and prickly pear of the desert, all in less than 2 miles.

Take a right at the Frijole Trail junction and continue to descend, albeit more gradually, toward Pine Springs. After 1.1 miles you hit the Foothills Trail, where you take a right and continue on the Frijole Trail as it heads west another 0.5 mile to the trailhead, passing through the two junctions you saw at the beginning of your hike.

Miles and Directions

0.0 Start at the Pine Springs trailhead.

0.1 At the Tejas Trail junction, turn left.

3.7 At the Bush Mountain Trail junction, turn right.

4.2 At the Middle Bowl Trail junction, turn right.

4.6 Pass a spur trail to the summit of Hunter Peak. **Option:** Climb the 0.25-mile spur trail to see the view from the top of Hunter Peak.

5.1 At the Bear Canyon Trail junction, turn right.

6.9 At the Frijole Trail junction, turn right.

8.0 At the Foothills Trail junction, turn right.

8.4 At the Tejas Trail junction, turn left.

8.5 Reach the Pine Springs trailhead.

22 The Bowl

Highlights: A good choice for an overnighter to the heart of the Guadalupe Mountains, but can also be a long day hike for the extra-fit hiker.
Start: Pine Springs trailhead.
Distance: 13.0-mile loop.

Difficulty: Difficult.
Maps: Trails Illustrated: Guadalupe Mountains; USGS: Guadalupe Peak; park brochure.
Trail contact: Guadalupe Mountains National Park, H.C. 60, Box 400, Salt Flat, TX 79847-9400; (915) 828-3251; www.nps.gov/gamo.

The Hike

This trip is, in essence, an elongated overnight version of the Hunter Peak Loop hike. Like the Hunter Peak Loop, this route is described in a clockwise manner.

Since you'll be staying overnight, you must choose your campsite before leaving and get the required backcountry permit from the Pine Springs Visitor Center. The first preference might be the Tejas campsite, which is as close as you can get to the midpoint of the trip. However, you can also stay at Pine Top, which is a short distance to your left once you reach the rim of the escarpment. If you plan on a late start on the first day and don't mind a long second day, you might prefer Pine Top. The Pine Top campground has six tent sites all leveled and squared, courtesy of the National Park Service. This campground has a better view than many other campsites in the park.

Begin your hike at the Pine Springs campground. Immediately after leaving the campground, you take a right at a major junction, with trails going off to the left to Guadalupe Peak and El Capitan and straight to Devil's Hall. You go right on the Frijole Trail. Then, in another 200 yards or so, after crossing the expansive dry wash of Pine Springs Canyon, you hit another junction with the Frijole Trail going straight. Turn left and head north up the hill on the Tejas Trail. You'll be coming back down the Frijole Trail.

The next mile is nearly flat with an almost imperceptible increase in elevation. Then, you start a moderate climb up to Pine Top, about 2,000 vertical feet over 3 miles of well-designed trail that minimizes the impact of the elevation gain. This is not an easy hike, even though the trail is as good as a trail can be. Plan on two to three hours to get to Pine Top—and longer if you have a heavy pack.

At the top of the big climb up from Pine Springs, you hit a crossroads–type junction where you can go all four directions. If you plan to stay overnight at Pine Top, the campground is 0.2 mile to your left when you enter the forest. You will have to retrace your steps back to the Tejas Trail in the morning. If you prefer to stay overnight at the Tejas campsite, go straight (north), staying on the Tejas Trail. The next 1.5 miles pass through the beautiful relict forest of the Guadalupe high country. You drop down about 300 feet in elevation along the way.

The narrow and steep Bear Canyon Trail.

The Tejas campsite is 0.3 mile past the Juniper Trail junction on the left (west) side of the trail. It has four tent sites. From tent site number 1, you get a good view of an old water tank, part of the historic water system used by ranchers to facilitate livestock grazing in the Bowl.

The next morning you retrace the 0.3 mile on the Tejas Trail to the Juniper Trail junction and take a left onto the Juniper Trail. Like the section of the Tejas Trail, the Juniper Trail is just a wonderful walk in the woods. The trail is in great shape, and nature improves it with a carpet of pine needles and oak leaves. It has junipers, of course, but seemingly no more than many other trails in the Guadalupe high country.

Watch carefully for elk, the monarch of the Guadalupe Mountains, as the over-sized ungulates frequently hang out in this neck of the woods. In September and October you can often hear the drawn-out bugle of the bull elk as you hike through the deep forest of the Bowl.

Along the Juniper Trail you'll see frequent signs of the ancient water delivery system—several old water tanks and a pipe running along the trail. Instead of looking

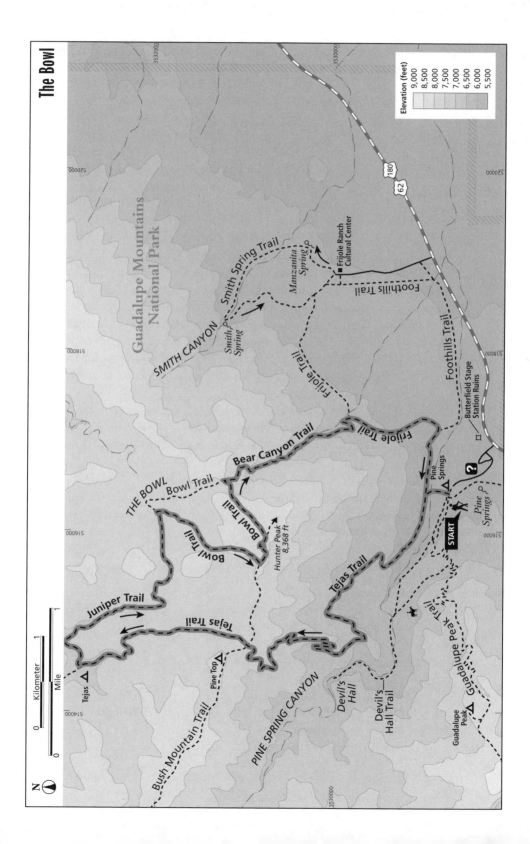

The Bowl

at the rusting pipes and tanks as eyesores on the unspoiled face of the wilderness, consider them lingering reminders of why we need national parks.

After 2 miles on the Juniper Trail, you hit a junction with the Bowl Trail. This forces a tough decision. You can complete the loop by going either left or right. Both trails go to the Bear Canyon Trail junction. Both trails continue to pass through the relict forest, with the Juniper Trail passing through a more open forest heavy with deciduous trees.

If you've already seen the view from Hunter Peak, you might try the left fork, which stays on the Juniper Trail for 0.8 mile before hitting the Bear Canyon Trail junction. This cuts 1 mile off your trip, unless you drop your pack at the Bear Canyon Trail junction and take a 1-mile side-trip up to the top of Hunter Peak and back.

If you haven't seen what has been called "the best view in Texas" from the top of Hunter Peak, you might want to take the longer route down the Bowl Trail. After a pleasant 0.9 mile, this trail hits the Bowl Trail, 0.4 mile from the short spur trail up to Hunter Peak, where you simply must drop your pack and take this 0.25-mile hike to the summit. After soaking in the view, go back to the Bowl Trail, take a right (east), and follow the Bowl Trail along the rim of the escarpment for another 0.5 mile to the Bear Canyon Trail junction, where you take a right. Some hikers might find this stretch of trail too steep to comfortably hike without slipping or feeling some pain in their knees, but it's short, only 1.8 miles to the junction with the Frijole Trail.

By the time you reach the Frijole Trail, you've seen a rapid change in the vegetation, going from the pine forest, through riparian vegetation like bigtooth maple, and then out into the yucca and prickly pear of the desert, all in less than 2 miles.

Take a right at the Frijole Trail junction and continue to descend, albeit more gradually, toward Pine Springs. After 1.1 miles, you hit the Foothills Trail where you take a right and continue on the Frijole Trail as it heads west another 1.5 miles to the Tejas Trail junction. Turn left here to reach the Pine Springs trailhead.

Miles and Directions

0.0 Start at the Pine Springs trailhead.

0.1 At the Tejas Trail junction, turn left.

3.7 At the Bush Mountain Trail junction, go straight. **Option:** If staying overnight at Pine Top, turn left and continue 0.2 mile to the campground. Return to Tejas Trail.

5.2 At the junction with Juniper Trail, go straight.

5.5 Reach the Tejas campsite. Retrace your way back to the Tejas Trail.

5.8 At the junction with Juniper Trail, turn left.

7.8 At the junction with Bowl Trail, turn right. **Option:** Take the left fork and continue on the Juniper Trail for 0.8 mile to the Bear Canyon Trail junction. Turn right and continue as described below.

8.7 At the junction with Hunter Peak Trail, turn left.

9.1 Pass a spur trail to summit of Hunter Peak. **Side-trip:** Climb the 0.25-mile spur trail to see the view from the top of Hunter Peak.

9.6 At the Bear Canyon Trail junction, turn right.

11.4 At the Frijole Trail junction, turn right.

12.5 At the Foothills Trail junction, turn right.

12.9 At the Tejas Trail junction, turn left.

13.0 Reach the Pine Springs trailhead.

23 Smith Spring

Highlights: A short hike to a rare desert oasis.
Start: Frijole Ranch.
Distance: 2.3-mile loop.
Difficulty: Easy to moderate.

Maps: Trails Illustrated: Guadalupe Mountains; USGS: Guadalupe Peak; park brochure.
Trail contact: Guadalupe Mountains National Park, H.C. 60, Box 400, Salt Flat, TX 79847-9400; (915) 828-3251; www.nps.gov/gamo.

Finding the trailhead: Drive north from the main entrance to Guadalupe Mountains National Park on U.S. Highway 62/180 for 1 mile and turn (left) north. The turnoff is well signed as FRIJOLE RANCH. Head up the well-maintained gravel road for about 0.5 mile until it dead-ends at the historic ranch and museum.

The Hike

For somebody who wants a short, easy hike that really captures the essence and diversity of the desert environment, the Smith Spring loop is ideal. It's only 2.3 miles with slight elevation gain, and it goes to lush and beautiful Smith Spring, which probably comes closer to fitting the stereotypical image of a desert oasis than any other place in the Guadalupe Mountains. The first 0.2 mile of the trail to Manzanita Spring is hardened and wheelchair accessible.

You can hike the loop either way, of course, but the counterclockwise option is described here. This route allows you to start out on the easiest section of the trail and visit Manzanita Spring only 0.2 mile after leaving the trailhead. To take the counterclockwise route, do not take the trail just on the left of the sign at the trailhead. Instead take the trail at the north edge of the ranch and museum.

The trail to Manzanita Spring is accessible to people with mobility impairments, and it's very easy walking. Watch for elk, deer, and other wildlife on this trip. The wild residents of the Guadalupe Mountains use the springs to quench their desert thirst. Try to plan the trip for evening to increase your chances of seeing wildlife.

Manzanita Spring is a marshy pond that's used heavily by wildlife as a water source, witnessed by the omnipresent animal tracks around the spring. This is also the site of a horrific attack on the Mescalero Apache in 1878, when Lt. Howard

Manzanita Spring with Nipple Hill in the background.

Cushing destroyed a large winter cache of food, probably resulting in the winter starvation of tribal members who managed to escape the raid.

After Manzanita Spring the trail gradually climbs to Smith Spring along Smith Canyon, a gorgeous desert riparian zone. On the 0.9-mile trail between the two springs, you can observe the aftermath of the 6,012-acre Frijole Fire of 1990, caused by lightning. You can see how some vegetation has made a comeback, but you can also see how slowly nature heals the land in the desert environment.

Smith Spring is an extraordinary oasis in the desert that literally springs out of the permeable limestone of the Guadalupe Mountains. So much water seeps out of the rock that it forms a small waterfall and a live stream.

Smith Spring is shaded by maidenhair fern, bigtooth maple, chinkepin oak, and Texas madrone. Imagine a fern in the middle of the Chihuahuan Desert!

The water in Smith Spring certainly looks good enough to drink, but please don't do it. It's against National Park Service regulations, and the water is unsuitable for human consumption. You get the bonus of leaving Smith Spring by gingerly stepping on well-placed stones to cross the stream with dry feet.

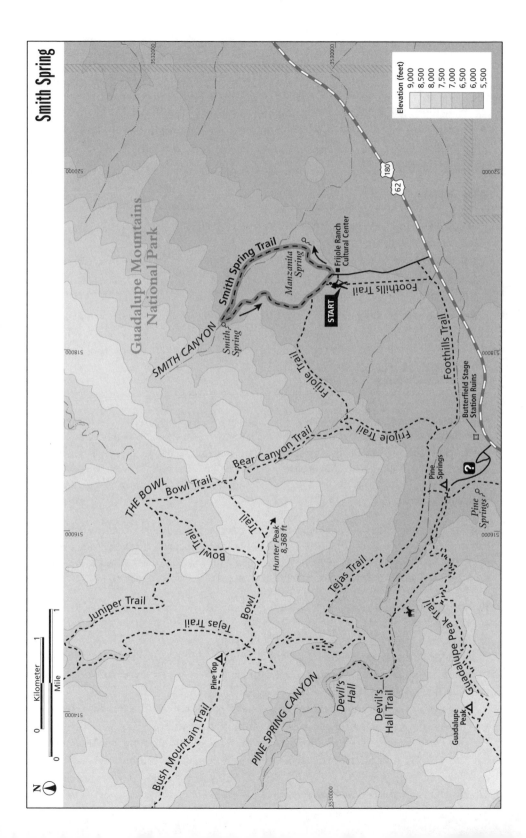

Smith Spring

N

Elevation (feet)
9,000
8,500
8,000
7,500
7,000
6,500
6,000
5,500

Kilometer
Mile

Guadalupe Mountains National Park

Smith Spring Trail

SMITH CANYON

Smith Spring

Manzanita Spring

Frijole Ranch Cultural Center

START

Foothills Trail

Frijole Trail

Bear Canyon Trail

THE BOWL

Bowl Trail

Bowl Trail

Bowl Trail

Hunter Peak 8,368 ft

Juniper Trail

Tejas Trail

Pine Top

PINE SPRING CANYON

Bush Mountain Trail

Frijole Trail

Foothills Trail

Butterfield Stage Station Ruins

Pine Springs

Pine Springs

Tejas Trail

Devil's Hall

Devil's Hall Trail

Guadalupe Peak Trail

Guadalupe Peak

180

62

Both Smith and Manzanita Springs are very fragile, so please observe at a distance, especially at Smith Spring. Stay in the fenced viewing area.

On the way back to the Frijole Ranch, you get a great view of Manzanita Spring with a distinct, cone-shaped landmark called Nipple Hill as a backdrop.

After 0.9 mile of easy downhill walking, the Frijole Trail heads off to the west. Shortly thereafter you'll see another junction that heads south to the Foothills Trail. Take a left at both junctions, and after another 0.3 mile you're back in the Frijole Ranch parking lot.

Miles and Directions

0.0 Start on the trail at the north edge of the ranch and museum.
0.2 Reach Manzanita Spring.
1.1 Reach Smith Spring.
2.0 At the junction with Frijole Trail, turn left.
2.2 At the junction with Foothills Trail, turn left.
2.3 Arrive at Frijole Ranch.

24 Foothills

Highlights: A convenient loop hike through the flatter sections of the park.
Start: Frijole Ranch or Pine Springs trailhead.
Distance: 4.5-mile loop (or could be a short shuttle).
Difficulty: Moderate.

Maps: Trails Illustrated: Guadalupe Mountains; USGS: Guadalupe Peak; park brochure.
Trail contact: Guadalupe Mountains National Park, H.C. 60, Box 400, Salt Flat, TX 79847-9400; (915) 828-3251; www.nps.gov/gamo.

Finding the trailhead: Drive north from the main entrance to Guadalupe Mountains National Park on U.S. Highway 62/180 for 1 mile and turn (left) north. The turnoff is well signed as FRIJOLE RANCH. Head up the well-maintained gravel road for about 0.5 mile until it dead-ends at the historic ranch and museum. You can also start this hike at the Pine Springs trailhead.

The Hike

You can take this loop from either the Frijole Ranch or the Pine Springs trailhead. However, starting at Pine Springs means 1 mile of additional hiking to get to and from the Foothills Trail. This trail description follows the clockwise route starting from the Frijole Ranch.

From the Frijole Ranch parking lot, take the main trail heading north from the parking lot and turn left after about 50 feet onto the Foothills Trail as it turns south.

The first 0.6 mile of the trail follows the gravel road leading from Frijole Ranch back to US 62/180. Then it turns right (west) and parallels the highway, but at a

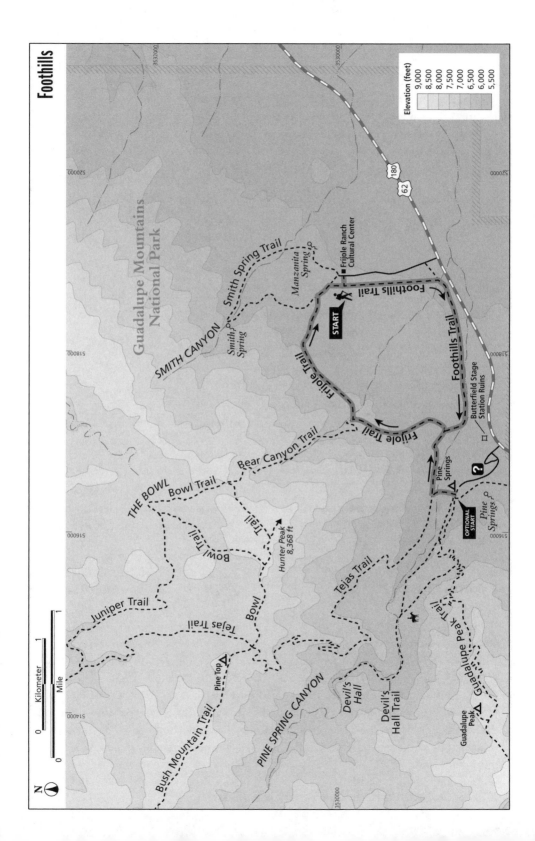

Foothills

Guadalupe Mountains National Park

SMITH CANYON

Smith Spring Trail

Manzanita Spring

Frijole Ranch Cultural Center

Smith Spring

Frijole Trail

START

Foothills Trail

Foothills Trail

Butterfield Stage Station Ruins

Frijole Trail

Bear Canyon Trail

THE BOWL

Bowl Trail

Bowl Trail

Bowl Trail

Hunter Peak 8,368 ft

Pine Springs

OPTIONAL START

Pine Springs

Juniper Trail

Tejas Trail

Tejas Trail

Bush Mountain Trail

Pine Top

Bowl

Tejas Trail

PINE SPRING CANYON

Devil's Hall

Devil's Hall Trail

Guadalupe Peak Trail

Guadalupe Peak

62

180

N

Kilometer   1

0

Mile   1

0

Elevation (feet)

9,000
8,500
8,000
7,500
7,000
6,500
6,000
5,500

tolerable distance. The roads and the power lines along the first 1.9 miles of this trail may seem like unwelcome distractions, but you can probably forget the intrusions by watching deer, which seem to be everywhere along this trail.

After 1.3 miles of paralleling the highway, you reach the junction with the Frijole Trail. Take a right (north) and start a gradual climb toward the mouth of Bear Canyon. After 1.1 miles the Bear Canyon Trail climbs northward to the Guadalupe high country. You turn right (east) and stay on the Frijole Trail, which levels out and goes 1.2 miles in the shadow of the escarpment. This is probably the nicest part of the loop. You get good views of the Frijole Ranch and the Pine Springs vicinity. Then you meet up with the Smith Spring Trail about 0.3 mile from the Frijole Ranch. Turn left, and it's only 0.3 mile to the parking lot.

For the shuttle option, start at either Frijole Ranch or Pine Springs and either leave a vehicle at the other trailhead or arrange to be picked up there.

Miles and Directions

0.0   Start on the main trail heading north from the Frijole Ranch parking lot.

0.1   At the junction with Foothills Trail, turn left.

1.9   At the junction with Frijole Trail, turn right.

3.0   Pass the junction with Bear Canyon Trail.

4.2   At the junction with Smith Spring Trail, turn right.

4.5   Turn left to arrive at the Frijole Ranch parking lot.

25 Bush Mountain

Highlights: A classic backpacking trip through the heartland of the Guadalupe Mountains.
Start: Pine Springs trailhead.
Distance: 17.8-mile loop (actually a figure eight).
Difficulty: Difficult.

Maps: Trails Illustrated: Guadalupe Mountains; USGS: Guadalupe Peak and PX Flat; park brochure.
Trail contact: Guadalupe Mountains National Park, H.C. 60, Box 400, Salt Flat, TX 79847-9400; (915) 828-3251; www.nps.gov/gamo.

The Hike

This loop trail offers an ideal multiday adventure in the remote regions of the Guadalupe Mountains—and also the opportunity to see the most famous features of the park, such as Guadalupe Peak and "the best view in Texas" from the summit of Hunter Peak. This trip has an advantage over other multiday backpacking treks in the Guadalupe Mountains. It's a loop and doesn't require shuttling a vehicle to the other trailhead or arranging a ride. Be sure to get your backcountry camping permit before hitting the trail.

The salt flats viewed from the Bush Mountain Trail.

Three days and two nights (at Bush Mountain and Tejas camps) is just right for this loop. This splits up nicely into a 6-mile segment for each day.

Well-conditioned hikers on a tight schedule can reduce the trip to two days, staying overnight at the Blue Ridge camp at approximately the halfway point, but this means two strenuous 9-mile days—especially the first day, which is mostly uphill. You can also take four days, staying three nights (probably at Pine Top, Blue Ridge, and again at Pine Top), and enjoy a relaxed pace that will give you ample time for side-trips and to fully enjoy the Guadalupe high country. In any case, be sure to take plenty of water.

As with the Hunter Peak loop hike, you could take the lower loop of this figure-eight hike counterclockwise instead of clockwise, but it would mean a very steep climb up Bear Canyon with a big pack, which is only recommended for hikers who want as much exercise as possible. Counterclockwise is easier on the knees, but clockwise is easier on the lungs. The upper loop of the figure eight can be done in either direction. The clockwise route seems only slightly easier because of the gradual climbs as opposed to the shorter, steeper climbs found on the counter-clockwise route, especially the climb (about 800 feet in a mile of trail) just east of

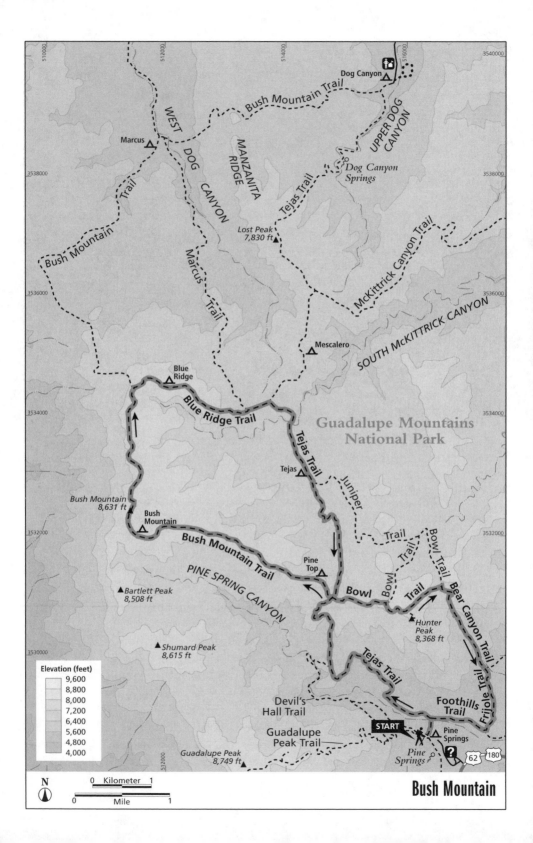

Bush Mountain

the Blue Ridge camp. The clockwise route for both loops is used for this trail description.

Immediately after leaving Pine Springs campground, you take a right at a major junction, with trails going off to the left to Guadalupe Peak and El Capitan and straight to Devil's Hall. You go right on the Frijole Trail. Then, in another 200 yards or so, after crossing the expansive dry wash of Pine Springs Canyon, you hit another junction with the Frijole Trail going straight. Turn left and head north up the hill on the Tejas Trail.

From the Pine Springs trailhead, it's a steady uphill grind to the top of the escarpment, accounting for most of the elevation gain on this multiday trip (almost 2,000 feet in 3.7 miles). From this point on you can expect only minor elevation gain and short hills. At this point you're entering the "high country," and you remain there the rest of the trip until you plunge down Bear Canyon.

If you started late in the day and plan at least a two-night trip, you can stay at Pine Top camp, 0.2 mile to your left on the Bush Mountain Trail just beyond the junction you'll find immediately after cresting the rim of the escarpment. Pine Top camp has six tent sites and a great view. Plan on two to three hours to get to Pine Top—and longer if you have a heavy pack.

If you started early in the day and plan two nights out, you might want to push on to the Bush Mountain camp, which has five tent sites and is nestled under a grove of huge Douglas fir and ponderosa pine. It's a short walk to the edge of the escarpment, with great sunset views to the west.

From the top of the escarpment, the Bush Mountain Trail climbs steadily for the first mile, gaining about 500 feet. It closely follows the steep edge of Pine Springs Canyon, offering incredible views of the expansive canyon and Guadalupe, Shumard, and Bartlett peaks.

The trail continues to climb, gradually, past Bush Mountain camp, to the top of 8,631-foot Bush Mountain, the second-highest peak in the park and all of Texas. The high-country forest stays with you all the way, even as you crest the summit of Bush Mountain, making the climb seem gentle. The serenity of the wilderness is broken briefly by a misplaced radio repeater station on top of Bush Mountain. However, you can quickly forget that minor intrusion by soaking in the extraordinary view of the salt flats, nearly 4,000 feet below, from an overlook near the top of Bush Mountain.

About 1.9 miles past the summit of Bush Mountain, you hit the Blue Ridge Trail junction. Turn right (east) here and go another 0.5 mile to the Blue Ridge camp on your left. If you're out for only one night, this is your best campsite. Like Bush Mountain camp, Blue Ridge camp has five sites and is shaded by stately Douglas fir and ponderosa pine, plus a few large oak trees.

From Bush Mountain camp, all along the Blue Ridge Trail, and on to the Tejas camp, you hike through the diversity of the relict forest of the Guadalupe Mountains. Watch for deer, elk, turkey, and other wildlife along the way—or take an early-morning or late-evening stroll from camp when the local residents are more active.

After a mile or so of fairly level—and very enjoyable—hiking on the Blue Ridge, you drop down a steep, rocky section to the Marcus Trail junction, where you turn right (east) and continue on another 0.3 mile to the Tejas Trail. Here, turn right (south) on the Tejas Trail and go another 0.8 mile to the Tejas camp, following a beautiful (and usually dry) streambed much of the way.

If you're out for two nights, the Tejas camp is probably your best choice for a second campsite. The Tejas camp has four tent sites, with number 1 offering the best view.

After leaving the Tejas camp, you quickly reach the junction with the Juniper Trail. You can take this alternative route back to Bear Canyon, but you'll miss Hunter Peak. So turn right at this junction and drop into the streambed for about a half mile before climbing out into the high-country forest all the way back to the center of your figure-eight route, the junction with the Bush Mountain and Bowl Trails. At this junction you can bail out early and head back down the Tejas Trail to Pine Springs, but this only cuts a mile off your trip, and you'll miss some of the best scenery. So instead turn left (east) to follow the Bowl Trail along the rim of the escarpment past Hunter Peak for 1.4 miles to the Bear Canyon Trail junction.

After 0.5 mile on the Bowl Trail, it splits. Turn right at the Middle Bowl Trail junction and continue going east along the edge of the cliff. Be sure to make a lengthy stop at Hunter Peak. Watch for the spur trail heading off to the right 0.4 mile after the split. Leave your pack behind and climb the 0.25 mile to the summit of Hunter Peak for a great view of Guadalupe Peak, El Capitan, and the surrounding area. Back on the Bowl Trail, it's another 0.5 mile to the Bear Canyon Trail junction, where you take a right. This stretch of trail is very steep, but short—only 1.8 miles to the junction with the Frijole Trail.

Take a right at the Frijole Trail junction and continue to descend, albeit more gradually, toward Pine Springs. After 1.1 miles, you hit the Foothills Trail where you take a right and continue on the Frijole Trail as it heads west another 1.5 miles to the Tejas Trail junction. Turn left here to reach the Pine Springs trailhead.

Miles and Directions

- **0.0** Start at the Pine Springs trailhead.
- **0.1** At the Tejas Trail junction, turn left.
- **3.7** At the Bush Mountain Trail junction, turn left.
- **3.9** Reach the Pine Top camp.
- **6.2** Reach the Bush Mountain camp.
- **6.5** Crest the summit of Bush Mountain.
- **8.4** At the Blue Ridge Trail junction, turn right.
- **8.9** Reach the Blue Ridge camp.
- **10.1** At the Marcus Trail junction, turn right.
- **10.4** At the Tejas Trail junction, turn right.

11.2 Reach the Tejas camp.

11.5 At the Juniper Trail junction, turn right. **Option:** Turn left for an alternative route back to Bear Canyon. Continue as described below.

13.0 At the Bush Mountain Trail junction, turn left onto the Bowl Trail. **Bail-out:** Go straight instead and follow the Tejas Trail all the way down to Pine Springs. (FYI: This only saves you 1 mile and is much less scenic.)

13.5 At the the Middle Bowl Trail junction, turn right.

13.9 Pass a spur trail to summit of Hunter Peak. **Side-trip:** Climb the 0.25-mile spur trail to see the view from the top of Hunter Peak.

14.4 At the Bear Canyon Trail junction, turn right.

16.2 At the Frijole Trail junction, turn right.

17.3 At the Foothills Trail junction, turn right.

17.7 At the Tejas Trail junction, turn left.

17.8 Reach the Pine Springs trailhead.

26 Pine Springs to McKittrick Canyon

Highlights: A classic trans-park route lined with the most scenic vistas in the entire Guadalupe Mountains.
Start: Pine Springs trailhead.
Distance: 18.9-mile shuttle.
Difficulty: Moderate, but long enough to be difficult.

Maps: Trails Illustrated: Guadalupe Mountains; USGS: Guadalupe Peak and PX Flat; park brochure.
Trail contact: Guadalupe Mountains National Park, H.C. 60, Box 400, Salt Flat, TX 79847-9400; (915) 828-3251; www.nps.gov/gamo.

The Hike

This trail slices through the heart of the Guadalupe Mountains and exposes many of its famous jewels to hikers lucky enough to take the trip. It includes views of Guadalupe Peak, a great walk in the woods through the relict high-altitude forest, vistas from the summit of Hunter Peak (with a short side-trip), McKittrick Canyon's famed viewpoint called the Notch, and the historic lodges and the natural wonders of McKittrick Canyon. If you have three days to see the Guadalupe Mountains, you couldn't spend the time much better.

You could do this trip in two days, but they would be two long days. This trail description covers the three-day, two-night option.

The first step is arranging transportation. The best option is leaving a vehicle at McKittrick Canyon Visitor Center. Because of the arduous climb to the top of McKittrick Ridge coming from the other direction, you won't want to do this trip in reverse. The big climb also makes it marginal for the "trading keys" option because a fight would likely break out over who has to start at the McKittrick Canyon trailhead.

Stepping stones where the trail crosses over McKittrick Canyon Creek help to preserve water quality.

When transportation has been arranged and you've obtained your backcountry camping permit, start your adventure at the Pine Springs trailhead. Immediately beyond Pine Springs campground, turn right on the Frijole Trail at the major junction with trails going off to the left to Guadalupe Peak and El Capitan and straight to Devil's Hall. Then, in another 0.25 mile, after crossing the large dry wash of Pine Springs Canyon, you hit another junction with the Tejas Trail. Turn left and head north up the hill on the Tejas Trail.

The next mile is nearly flat with an almost indiscernible increase in elevation. Then you start a moderate climb to Pine Top, gaining almost 2,000 feet over 3 miles of well-designed trail that minimizes the impact of the climb. This trail is as good as a trail can be, but it still doesn't make this an easy hike, especially on a hot day with your big pack heavy with a three-day water supply.

Depending on how late in the day you hit the trail and the availability of backcountry permits, you have the choice of spending the first night at Pine Top or Tejas camp. Tejas camp is better situated at 5.5 miles into your hike, leaving 5.8 miles and

7.6 miles, respectively, for the second and third day of the trip. If you stay at Pine Top, you leave 7.6 miles for each of the last two days of the trip.

Pine Top camp has six tent sites and a great view. Tejas camp has four tent sites, and the view doesn't match that of Pine Top, but it provides better shelter from the wind. To reach Pine Top camp, you climb 0.2 mile to the left on the Bush Mountain Trail when you reach the junction at the rim of the escarpment—and then retrace your steps to the junction the next morning, lengthening your trip by about a half mile.

The trail between the two camps passes through the deep forest of the Guadalupe Mountains as it gradually descends to Tejas camp. Just before Tejas camp, you'll see the Juniper Trail veering off to the right. Go straight (north), staying on the Tejas Trail.

About 0.8 mile beyond Tejas camp, the Blue Ridge Trail branches off to the left. Stay on the Tejas Trail. In another 0.7 mile you'll see the Mescalero camp on your right. This is a great campsite with eight tent sites, but it's poorly located for a three-day trip. For a two-day trip the Mescalero camp would be your best choice for your overnight stay.

In 0.8 mile you reach the junction with the McKittrick Canyon Trail. Here you leave the Tejas Trail and turn right (east) on the McKittrick Canyon Trail. From Pine Top to the McKittrick Trail junction, the trail has stayed in the forest, but on McKittrick Ridge the forest opens up and treats you to magnificent vistas in all directions for the next 5 miles. On your right you have the complete wildness of South McKittrick Canyon, which has been totally preserved by the National Park Service, with no entry allowed.

Along the way, about 3.5 miles after the junction, you'll see the McKittrick Ridge camp on your left, your campsite for the second night out. McKittrick Ridge camp has eight tent sites. Numbers 1 and 8 offer the most privacy. About the only place on McKittrick Ridge where you can't get a great view is from the camp, which is off the trail in a fairly dense stand of junipers, Douglas fir, and ponderosa pine.

After you leave McKittrick Ridge camp the next morning, it's all downhill. You stay on the ridge for about 1.5 miles and then start down the big drop into the colorful bottomlands of McKittrick Canyon. Here is where you're glad you took the author's advice and didn't do the trip in reverse.

While hiking through McKittrick Canyon, be sure to stop at the Grotto and Hunter Line Cabin about 4 miles from the camp (follow the spur trail) and Pratt Lodge another mile down the trail. Just before Pratt Lodge you're suddenly exposed to a very rare sight in the Guadalupe Mountains—a free-flowing stream that surfaces here and there along the last 3 miles of the trail. McKittrick Canyon Creek is an extremely precious resource, and park regulations prohibit entering the stream or using the water for any reason. You should remain on the established trail whenever it crosses over the stream.

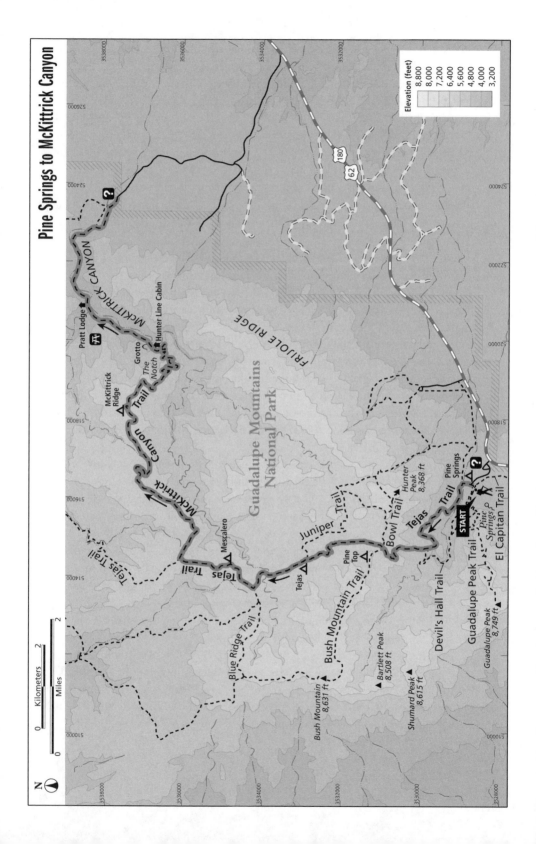

Pine Springs to McKittrick Canyon

Guadalupe Mountains National Park

The entire trip through McKittrick Canyon passes through a lush and diverse forest quite unlike the high-altitude forest of the Bowl. You'll definitely feel nature saved the best part for last, especially if you do this trip in the fall with McKittrick Canyon awash with the colors of autumn. Be sure to stay on the trail. Park regulations prohibit off-trail travel in McKittrick Canyon.

The McKittrick Canyon road closes at 6:00 P.M. while daylight savings time is in effect and 4:30 P.M. during standard time, so you must be out of the woods and on the road in time to reach U.S. Highway 62/180 before the NPS locks the gate.

Miles and Directions

0.0   Start at the Pine Springs trailhead.

0.1   At the junction with Tejas Trail, turn left.

3.7   At the junction with Bush Mountain Trail, go straight.

5.2   At the junction with Juniper Trail, turn left.

5.5   Arrive at the Tejas camp.

6.3   At the junction with Blue Ridge Trail, turn right.

7.0   Reach the Mescalero camp.

7.8   At the junction with McKittrick Canyon Trail, turn right.

11.3   Arrive at the McKittrick Ridge camp.

14.0   Reach the Notch.

15.4   Turn up the spur trail to the Grotto and Hunter Line Cabin. Return to the main trail.

16.5   Reach Pratt Lodge.

18.9   Finish at the McKittrick Canyon trailhead and visitor center.

McKittrick Canyon Trailhead

McKittrick Canyon shows up on lots of postcards and photo essays. It's a truly exquisite place and has even been called "the most beautiful spot in Texas."

As you drive by on U.S. Highway 62/180, you probably won't notice the mouth of the canyon. In fact, the hidden beauty of the canyon doesn't reveal itself until you're almost in it. A heavily used trail follows the streambed and then climbs out of the canyon and into the heart of the Guadalupe Mountains.

Named after Felix McKittrick, who ran cattle in the canyon around 1870, the canyon now endures as a tiny island of untamed nature. You can buy a brochure at the visitor center that fully explains the history of McKittrick Canyon.

Photographers who flock here in the fall when the maple, oak, and ash trees are ablaze with color revere the canyon. But the most unusual natural phenomenon of all is the permanent, spring-fed stream flowing out of the canyon—very rare in this arid corner of the world. Rainbow trout were introduced into the stream, and it still supports a small and struggling population.

The canyon is also famous for its diversity of plants and animals. For example, 58 mammal and 260 bird species have been seen in McKittrick Canyon, not to mention the unbelievable diversity of vegetation, a unique melding of high-altitude and desert plants. The canyon has gathered plants from all environments. It isn't just one beautiful place; it's part of several beautiful places.

It's also a fragile place. The National Park Service has imposed many regulations to protect it—no overnight camping, no pets, no wading in the stream, etc. Hikers must stay on the trail, and after the Grotto no entry at all is allowed in South McKittrick Canyon so as to completely protect it. McKittrick Canyon is an uncommon and naturally precious place. These regulations will keep it that way.

Finding the Trailhead

To find the trailhead, go north from the park headquarters at Pine Springs on US 62/180 for 8 miles until you see the well-signed turn into McKittrick Canyon. Turn west at this turn and follow the paved road 4.5 miles to the McKittrick Canyon Visitor Center parking lot. The trails start behind the visitor center.

View of McKittrick Canyon from the Notch. ▶

27 McKittrick Canyon Nature Trail

Highlights: A wonderful nature trail to help you find out about the local flora and fauna.
Start: McKittrick Canyon Visitor Center.
Distance: 0.9-mile loop.
Difficulty: Easy.

Maps: Trails Illustrated: Guadalupe Mountains; USGS: Guadalupe Peak and Independence Spring; park brochure.
Trail contact: Guadalupe Mountains National Park, H.C. 60, Box 400, Salt Flat, TX 79847-9400; (915) 828-3251; www.nps.gov/gamo.

The Hike

This trail is just right for a short, easy hike. Along the way you get a bonus—a chance to learn about many plants and animals inhabiting the McKittrick Canyon area.

The trail starts right at the visitor center. Take a left at the junction just past the center. In addition to seeing some great scenery at the entrance to the grand McKittrick Canyon, you learn all kinds of things—and enjoy doing it.

You'll learn why you should like rattlesnakes, how the oversized soaptree yucca depends on a tiny moth, that alligator juniper can grow as old as 800 years in this harsh environment, how javelinas depend on prickly pear pads for food and water, the favorite food of the local deer population, and the facts about the "century plant."

About twenty more interpretive signs tell you even more. You'll love this classroom.

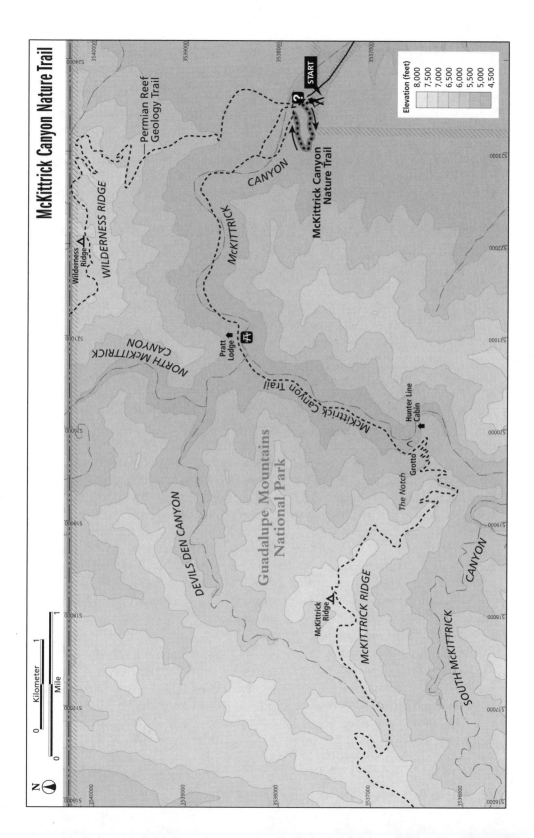

McKittrick Canyon Nature Trail

28 McKittrick Canyon

Highlights: A popular route through the famous McKittrick Canyon with lots of options.
Start: McKittrick Canyon Visitor Center.
Distance: 4.6 miles out and back to Pratt Lodge, 7 miles out and back to the Grotto, and 10.2 miles out and back to the Notch.
Difficulty: Easy to Pratt Lodge, moderate to the Grotto, and difficult to the Notch.
Maps: Trails Illustrated: Guadalupe Mountains; USGS: Guadalupe Peak and Independence Spring; park brochure.
Trail contact: Guadalupe Mountains National Park, H.C. 60, Box 400, Salt Flat, TX 79847-9400; (915) 828-3251; www.nps.gov/gamo.

The Hike

As you drive up the road toward McKittrick Canyon, you might not believe you're headed for one of most famous and scenic spots in Texas. The topography hides the canyon well.

Rest assured that McKittrick Canyon is a truly wonderful place, but don't plan on having it to yourself. This is probably is the most popular hike in the Guadalupe Mountains—and with good reason.

The trail meanders through a spectacular forest with a wide variety of conifers and deciduous trees. During autumn the maples, oaks, and other hardwoods burst into a world-famous kaleidoscopic panorama of fall colors. The trees are the same species found in other canyons in the park, but here they're bigger, and the entire forest seems more lush and majestic in the shadow of the steep cliffs on both sides of the canyon.

Hikers also get the rare opportunity to walk along a permanent desert stream—with a reproducing trout population. The stream appears and disappears several places along the first 3 miles of this hike. Please don't drink or wade in the stream. It's so special and rare and fragile that everybody must take the greatest care not to despoil it even in the slightest way.

About 2.3 miles up the trail, hikers can marvel at the grand old Pratt Lodge, so stately and nicely situated at the confluence of North McKittrick Canyon and South McKittrick Canyon that it inspires dreams of spending a few nights in this paradise. Sorry, though, the lodge is closed to the public. However, National Park Service volunteers often stay here to take care of the lodge and answer your questions—a "tough job" if you can afford it.

The first part of the trail is in embarrassingly good condition, double wide all the way and flat. It "climbs" inch by inch for a total of only 200 feet in elevation over 2.3 miles. The trail crosses the flowing stream twice on the way to Pratt Lodge.

The lodge is named for Wallace E. Pratt, a young geologist for Humble Oil Company (now ExxonMobil) who built the residence at the scenic confluence of North and South McKittrick Canyons in the 1920s and 1930s. He and his family

The first part of the excellent trail up McKittrick Canyon.

lived here off and on until 1957, when they donated 5,632 acres of their 16,000-acre ranch to the U.S. government for the beginnings of a national park. Pratt Lodge is a large stone building with several outbuildings. Of special note are the magnificent stone picnic tables and a historic stone fence surrounding the lodge.

Beyond the lodge the trail gets "normal." The stream surfaces again just down the trail from the lodge. The trail continues through the same forested environs for another 1.1 miles until a spur trail veers off to your left. Take this trail for about 0.1 mile to the Grotto, which is akin to a "surface cave" complete with speleoderms that look like they should be subterranean. This is also a good place for a lunch break on one of the stone picnic tables found here.

Just down the spur trail from the Grotto is the historic Hunter Line Cabin, where the spur trail ends. The cabin served as temporary quarters for ranch hands working the large Guadalupe Mountains Ranch owned by Judge J. C. Hunter and his son J. C. Hunter Jr. After the Hunter family sold it to the NPS, it became a major portion of the park.

South McKittrick Canyon beyond the Hunter Line Cabin has been preserved by the NPS as a Research Natural Area, with no entry allowed. If you're heading to the Notch, retrace your steps to the main trail and head up the canyon.

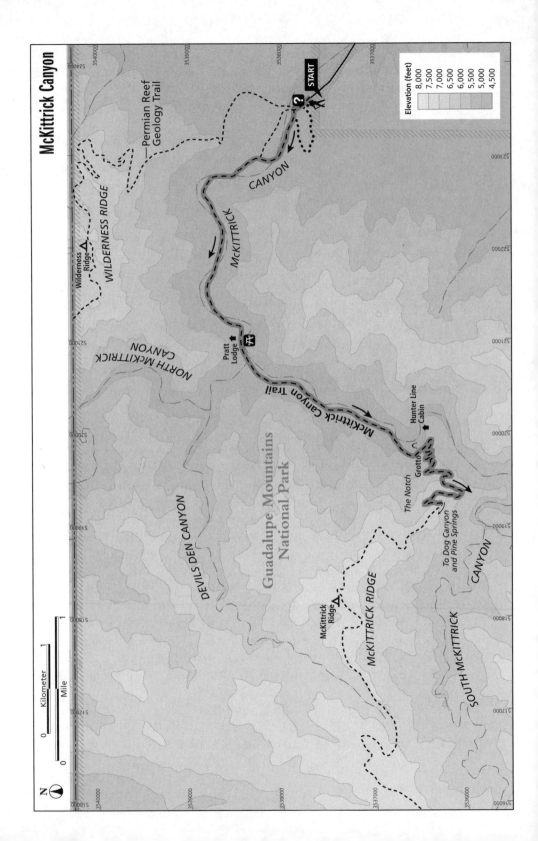

McKittrick Canyon

N

Elevation (feet)
8,000
7,500
7,000
6,500
6,000
5,500
5,000
4,500

Kilometer
0   1

Mile
0   1

START

Permian Reef Geology Trail

WILDERNESS RIDGE

Wilderness Ridge

NORTH McKITTRICK CANYON

McKITTRICK CANYON

Pratt Lodge

Guadalupe Mountains National Park

DEVILS DEN CANYON

McKittrick Canyon Trail

Hunter Line Cabin

Grotto

The Notch

McKittrick Ridge

McKITTRICK RIDGE

To Dog Canyon and Pine Springs

SOUTH McKITTRICK CANYON

The Hunter Line Cabin.

In a half mile or so, you reach the bottom of the toughest climb in Guadalupe Mountains National Park. The 2,600-foot ascent rivals any hill in the park, even the trip up to the summit of Guadalupe Peak. On a hot day you'll be glad you aren't carrying a big pack.

The trail switchbacks up the side of South McKittrick Canyon for about 1.5 miles, until it slips through a distinctive narrow spot in the cliff called the Notch. This is a perfect place to take a long break and absorb the extraordinary scenery you probably didn't notice as you climbed up here. Now you can sit down and look back down the canyon and see the Hunter Line Cabin, Pratt Lodge, and the multi-splendored forest surrounding them. The view is just as staggering as the trip up was. When you think about how hard it was to get to the Notch, you realize that you've only covered about half of the climb to the top of McKittrick Ridge.

After relaxing for a while, retrace your steps back to the visitor center. Be sure to leave enough time to get out to U.S. Highway 62/180, as the NPS closes the gate at 6:00 P.M. while daylight savings time is in effect and 4:30 P.M. during standard time.

Miles and Directions

0.0   Start at the McKittrick Canyon Visitor Center.

2.3   Arrive at Pratt Lodge. **Option:** Turn around here for the 4.6-mile out and back.

3.4   Follow a spur trail on the left to the Grotto and Hunter Line Cabin.

3.5   Reach the Grotto and Hunter Line Cabin. **Option:** Turn around here for the 7-mile out and back.

4.0   Begin the big climb.

5.1   Reach the Notch. Turn around and head back to the McKittrick Canyon Visitor Center.

29 McKittrick Ridge

Highlights: An overnight trip to a super-scenic ridgetop camp with all the amenities of McKittrick Canyon along the way.
Start: McKittrick Canyon Visitor Center.
Distance: 15.2 miles out and back.
Difficulty: Difficult.

Maps: Trails Illustrated: Guadalupe Mountains; USGS: Guadalupe Peak and Independence Spring; park brochure.
Trail contact: Guadalupe Mountains National Park, H.C. 60, Box 400, Salt Flat, TX 79847-9400; (915) 828-3251; www.nps.gov/gamo.

The Hike

Be sure to get a backcountry camping permit at the visitor center. Then head out on the McKittrick Canyon Trail. The trail meanders through a spectacular forest of varied conifers and deciduous trees. Hikers on this trail also get the opportunity to walk along a permanent desert stream, which is the habitat for a reproducing trout population. The stream appears and disappears several places along the first 3 miles of this hike. Please don't drink or wade in this rare and fragile stream. It's so special that everyone must take the greatest care not to despoil it in any way.

About 2.3 miles up the trail, hikers can admire the grand old Pratt Lodge, situated at the confluence of North McKittrick Canyon and South McKittrick Canyon. Pratt Lodge is a large stone building with several outbuildings. Of special note are the magnificent stone picnic tables and a historic stone fence surrounding the lodge. The lodge is closed to the public, but NPS volunteers often stay there to take care of the lodge and answer your questions.

The first part of the trail is flat and double wide all the way. It "climbs" inch by inch for a total of only 200 feet in elevation over 2.3 miles. The trail crosses the flowing stream twice on the way to Pratt Lodge. Beyond the lodge the trail gets "normal." The stream surfaces again just down the trail from the lodge.

Steps carved out of solid rock help hikers get up the big hill to McKittrick Ridge. ▶

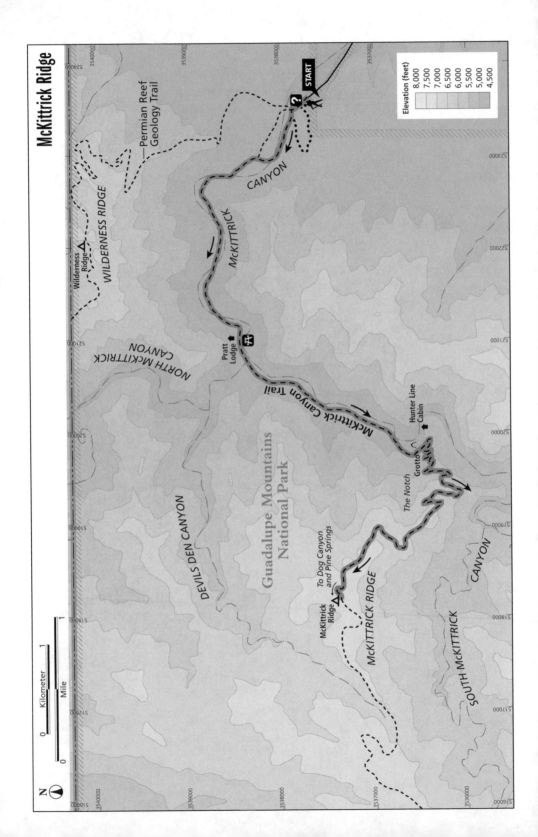

McKittrick Ridge

Elevation (feet)
- 8,000
- 7,500
- 7,000
- 6,500
- 6,000
- 5,500
- 5,000
- 4,500

Permian Reef Geology Trail

WILDERNESS RIDGE

Wilderness Ridge

START

McKITTRICK CANYON

NORTH McKITTRICK CANYON

Pratt Lodge

McKittrick Canyon Trail

Hunter Line Cabin

The Notch

Grotto

DEVILS DEN CANYON

Guadalupe Mountains National Park

To Dog Canyon and Pine Springs

McKittrick Ridge

McKITTRICK RIDGE

SOUTH McKITTRICK CANYON

N

Kilometer

Mile

The trail continues through the same forested environs for another 1.1 miles until a spur trail veers off to your left. Take this trail for about 0.1 mile to the Grotto. Just down the spur trail from the Grotto is the historic Hunter Line Cabin, where the spur trail ends. South McKittrick Canyon beyond the Hunter Line Cabin has been preserved by the NPS as a Research Natural Area, with no entry allowed. If you're heading to the Notch, retrace your steps to the main trail and head up the canyon. Here the trail changes dramatically. It's no longer the serene walk in the woods of the McKittrick Canyon bottomlands. It's quite the other extreme.

After about 4 miles of easy walking, the trail starts climbing up what could be called "the Big Sweat." It's as steep a climb as you'll find on any established trail. You gain about 2,600 feet in elevation in about 4 miles. Most of this elevation gain (about 1,600 feet) occurs in the first 1.5 miles. The grade eases slightly after you go through the Notch, where the trail passes through a distinctive narrowing of the canyon walls.

Since the climb starts 4 miles from the trailhead, it's difficult to do early in the morning to take advantage of cooler temperatures. Therefore, unfortunately, it's usually hot and always steep. This means you need to carry lots of water.

It's a vicious circle. You need to carry lots of water, which makes your pack heavier, which means you go slower and work harder, which means you dip into the hottest part of the day, which means you sweat more, which means you need to carry lots of water.

It's best to plan for a whole day on the trail. Go slowly and take lots of rest stops to take in the scenery, which is fantastic. From several points on the trail, you can marvel at the size and beauty of McKittrick Canyon.

After about 2.5 miles you lose some of your view into McKittrick Canyon, as the trail slips into a forested environment. You're still climbing, though, but not as steeply, for another 1.5 miles or so until you see the McKittrick Ridge camp on your right.

The McKittrick Ridge camp has eight tent sites, with numbers 1 and 8 offering the most privacy. You don't get the same panoramic view from the camp as you had during the last half of your hike up to the camp, but you can satisfy that need by hiking down the trail to the west for another 100 yards or so. The camp itself is nestled in a beautiful grove of ponderosa pine, Douglas fir, and junipers.

If you have any energy left after supper, take a short hike on the trail west from the camp along the ridgeline. The scenery is sensational, and you'll probably see deer and elk enjoying the last hours of sunlight.

After a relaxing evening and a good night's sleep at the McKittrick Ridge camp, retrace your steps back to the visitor center the next morning. Be sure to leave camp early enough to get out to U.S. Highway 62/180, as the NPS closes the gate at 6:00 P.M. while daylight savings time is in effect and 4:30 P.M. during standard time.

Miles and Directions

0.0 Start at the McKittrick Canyon Visitor Center.

2.3 Arrive at Pratt Lodge.

3.4 Follow a spur trail on the left to the Grotto and Hunter Line Cabin.

3.5 Reach the Grotto and Hunter Line Cabin.

4.0 Begin the big climb.

5.1 Reach the Notch.

7.6 Arrive at McKittrick Ridge camp. Turn around and head back to the visitor center.

30 Permian Reef

Highlights: A little-used but spectacular trail to a remote backcountry camp, excellent for either an overnighter or long day hike.
Start: McKittrick Canyon Visitor Center.
Distance: 8.4 miles out and back.
Difficulty: Difficult.

Maps: Trails Illustrated: Guadalupe Mountains; USGS: Guadalupe Peak and Independence Spring; park brochure.
Trail contact: Guadalupe Mountains National Park, H.C. 60, Box 400, Salt Flat, TX 79847-9400; (915) 828-3251; www.nps.gov/gamo.

The Hike

Permian Reef is one of the most spectacular trails in the park. Yet it doesn't receive much use. Most people going to McKittrick Canyon to hike choose the flat route up the beautiful, forested canyon, and who can blame them when the alternative is a 2,000-foot climb to Wilderness Ridge? For somebody who wants more exercise, though, this trail may be just as rewarding—and definitely less crowded. It can be a wonderful day-long hike or a great overnighter. If you're spending the night at the Wilderness Ridge camp, be sure to get a permit at the visitor center before leaving.

The trail does get heavy use from geology fans. In fact, the University of Texas–El Paso has a cooperative arrangement with the National Park Service to use the trail as an outdoor classroom. Key geological points are marked on the trail with twenty-eight metal signs. You can learn more about the geological story of the area by purchasing a book on the area at one of the park's visitor centers.

The trail starts out just past the visitor center. Take a right at the trail register and follow an old road for about 100 yards through and along the dry wash of McKittrick Canyon Creek, until you see the sign where the Permian Reef Trail starts switchbacking up the canyon wall. The trail is very well constructed to minimize the impact of the climb, so if you're in good shape, you'll barely notice the elevation gain. There is one section about two thirds of the way up where the trail is etched out of the steep canyon wall. This section might be nerve-wracking for parents with young children.

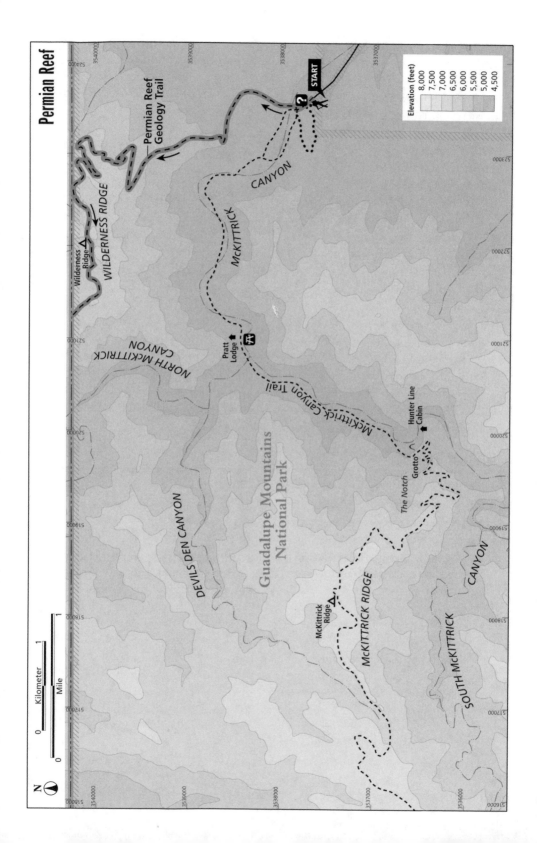

Permian Reef

Guadalupe Mountains National Park

Permian Reef Geology Trail

WILDERNESS RIDGE

Wilderness Ridge

McKITTRICK CANYON

NORTH McKITTRICK CANYON

DEVILS DEN CANYON

Pratt Lodge

McKittrick Canyon Trail

Hunter Line Cabin

The Notch

Grotto

McKITTRICK RIDGE

McKittrick Ridge

SOUTH McKITTRICK CANYON

START

N

Kilometer

Mile

Elevation (feet)

8,000
7,500
7,000
6,500
6,000
5,500
5,000
4,500

After you've climbed for a while, you can look down into McKittrick Canyon and clearly see where the stream suddenly disappears into the streambed, appears again momentarily, and then disappears again.

After a mile or so, on a little plateau, you'll see a geology loop trail veering off to the right. This is a special trail used for geology classes, so take a left, staying on the main route. The loop rejoins the main route a short way up the trail.

Between markers 4 and 5, the trail goes through a narrow slot. And at about the 2.5-mile point just past marker 15, it looks like you've reached the top of the ridge, but, sorry, it's a false summit. You're only slightly more than halfway to the ridgeline.

At about the 3.5-mile mark, you break out onto Wilderness Ridge, and the trail is flat the rest of the way. The vistas up here will stop you in your tracks.

Wilderness Ridge camp is on your right amid a few scattered ponderosa pines and junipers. It has five tent sites, and the scenery rivals that of any camp in the park. Beauty is always in the eye of the beholder, but this camp, along with Guadalupe Peak camp, would probably be voted the most scenic in the park by anybody who has seen all of them.

If you're staying overnight, you can take a hike that evening or the next morning for another 0.6 mile along Wilderness Ridge to the park boundary. The trail worsens slightly because of lack of use, but it's a beautiful walk. If you want more hiking, you can continue on outside of the park into the Lincoln National Forest.

Be sure you leave enough time to get down to the visitor center and then out to U.S. Highway 62/180 before 6:00 P.M. when daylight savings time is in effect and 4:30 P.M. during standard time, when the NPS locks the gate.

Miles and Directions

0.0 Start at McKittrick Canyon Visitor Center.

0.1 Trail leaves dry wash.

1.0 Stay on the main trail as you pass a geology loop trail on the right.

3.5 Reach Wilderness Ridge.

4.2 Arrive at Wilderness Ridge camp. **Option:** Continue along Wilderness Ridge for another 0.6 mile to the park boundary before turning around and heading back to the visitor center.

Dog Canyon Trailhead

Located just south of the New Mexico/Texas line, the Dog Canyon campground and trailhead is a remote jewel on the north edge of Guadalupe Mountains National Park. The other two trailheads (Pine Springs and McKittrick Canyon) receive heavy use, mainly because they are right along U.S. Highway 62/180. On the other hand, you have to put in some extra miles and effort to get to Dog Canyon. If you have an extra day, however, it's worth the trip.

The campground itself is a delightful combination of modern convenience and primitive beauty. You'll find a water fountain and toilet facilities, but there is also a nice array of native vegetation around the nine tent sites and more privacy than you might normally find in a developed campground. The campground has four parking spots for recreational vehicles (no hookups) and is used by both backpackers for overnight stays and tent campers who drive the 70 miles from Carlsbad, New Mexico. The trailhead is about 100 yards south of the campground.

You can usually see deer right from the tent sites, and if you get up early, you'll see the grand exodus of the local turkey vulture population, which roosts overnight on big snags just east of the campground.

Early settlers named this place Dog Canyon for the large population of black-tailed prairie dogs in the area. However, the unpopular rodents were exterminated long ago.

In 1994 a lightning-caused fire burned much of the area west of the campground. However, nature is rapidly reclaiming the area.

Finding the Trailhead

From Carlsbad, New Mexico, go north on U.S. Highway 285 for about 12 miles and turn left (west) on New Mexico Highway 137. Stay on NM 137 for about 58 miles until it ends at the Dog Canyon campground.

31 Indian Meadow Nature Trail

Highlights: A great after-dinner stroll with an interpretive brochure to help you learn about the local flora and fauna.
Start: Dog Canyon campground.
Distance: 0.6-mile loop.
Difficulty: Easy.

Maps: No map needed; use brochure available at trailhead.
Trail contact: Guadalupe Mountains National Park, H.C. 60, Box 400, Salt Flat, TX 79847-9400; (915) 828-3251; www.nps.gov/gamo.

The Hike

The Indian Meadow Nature Trail can be found by following a groomed trail (a five-minute walk) south from the water fountain in Dog Canyon campground.

Early settlers in the area saw tepees set up in this meadow and named it Indian Meadow. Today it's certainly easy to see why Native Americans used the meadow as a campsite. It's level, protected, and near water sources.

This isn't really a hike. It's an evening or early-morning stroll that offers an educational bonus—a series of twenty-five designated stops keyed to a free interpretive brochure available at the trailhead. The brochure describes the remarkable natural diversity of the area as well as its cultural history. It's certainly rare to be able to study so many aspects of natural and cultural history in one small spot—and in such a convenient location. This is a dirt trail with no hills, perfect for hikers interested in a short, easy stroll or for people unable to walk long distances.

You learn about native vegetation such as red berberis, alligator juniper, ponderosa pine, cane cholla, prickly pear, and desert rose; how the plants provide vital food and habitat for birds and mammals; how to watch for fascinating microhabitats; how water (or lack thereof) affects local plants and animals; how the area formed geologically; and how early residents and settlers adapted to the area.

As in all parts of the park, don't damage or collect any natural features. This is particularly important here, as so many people use this trail. If each person took one rock or flower, it would rapidly deface the gorgeous meadow.

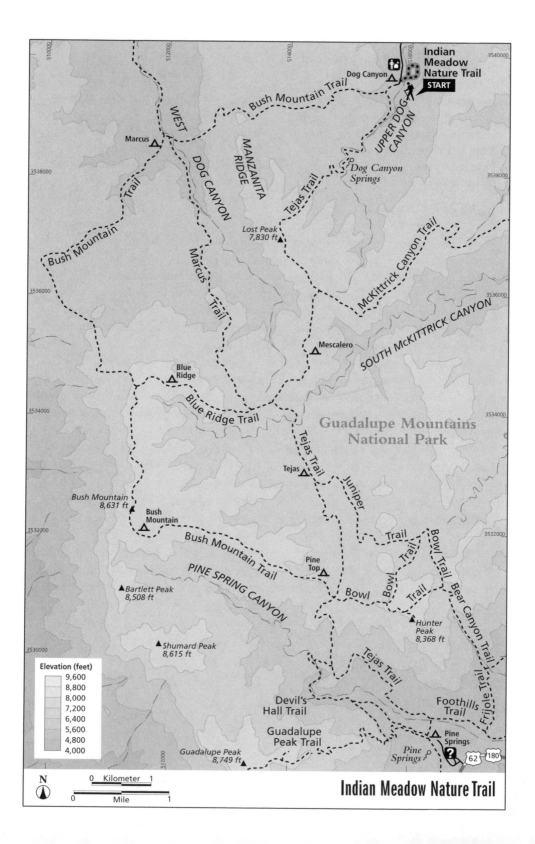

Indian Meadow Nature Trail

32 Lost Peak

Highlights: A nice day hike offering an opportunity to see how nature reclaims the landscape following a wildfire.
Start: Dog Canyon campground.
Distance: 6 miles out and back.
Difficulty: Moderate.

Maps: Trails Illustrated: Guadalupe Mountains; USGS: Guadalupe Peak; park brochure.
Trail contact: Guadalupe Mountains National Park, H.C. 60, Box 400, Salt Flat, TX 79847-9400; (915) 828-3251; www.nps.gov/gamo.

The Hike

For people staying at Dog Canyon campground, the Indian Meadow Nature Trail may not be enough exercise and excitement. If so, the Lost Peak Trail is a great choice for a half-day hike. It's a convenient distance (6 miles), and with a 1,400-foot elevation gain in 3 miles, you'll get enough exercise.

In 1994 a lightning-caused fire scorched much of the area right around the campground. You can see that nature has quickly reclaimed the surface, but it will take many years to replace some of the majestic trees killed in the fire.

The junction with the Bush Mountain Trail veers off to the right just after you leave the Dog Canyon trailhead. You go left and follow the Tejas Trail. Even though some sections of this trail were burned, it's still a pleasant hike, especially at dawn and dusk when the local residents (wild turkey, deer, and other wild animals) are out in force.

The trail gradually climbs for the first 1.5 miles, following Dog Canyon. Just before you get to Dog Canyon Springs, the trail takes a sharp right and starts a steep climb up to Lost Peak. Then, you switchback up the west side of Dog Canyon to a ridgeline where you get great views back to the campground area you just left. You gain most of the elevation in the next 1.5 miles, about 1,100 feet if you go all the way to the top of Lost Peak.

Watch your topo map so you don't hike right by Lost Peak. There's no sign. You'll notice it off to your right a short distance off the trail. You can scramble up to the top for the big view and then retrace your steps back to Dog Canyon trailhead.

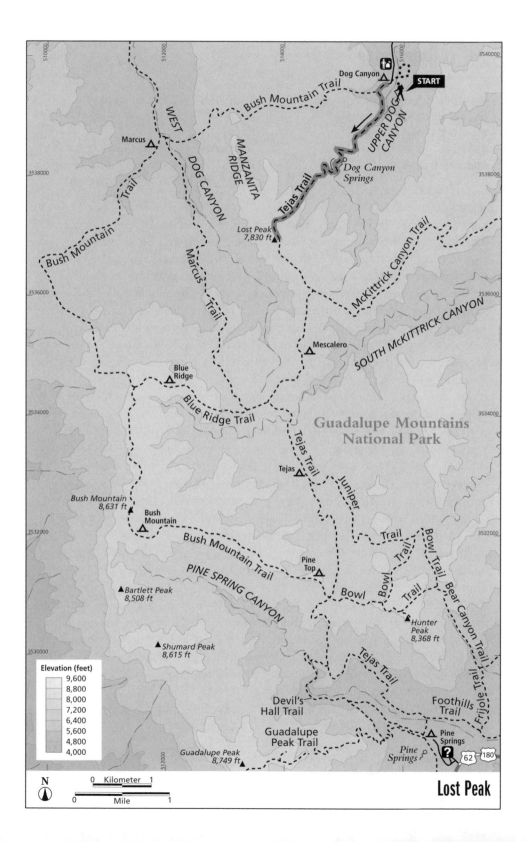

Lost Peak

33 Blue Ridge

Highlights: A serious trip for the adventurous and well-conditioned backpacker.
Start: Dog Canyon campground.
Distance: 14.8-mile loop.
Difficulty: Difficult.

Maps: Trails Illustrated: Guadalupe Mountains; USGS: Guadalupe Peak and PX Flat; park brochure.
Trail contact: Guadalupe Mountains National Park, H.C. 60, Box 400, Salt Flat, TX 79847-9400; (915) 828-3251; www.nps.gov/gamo.

The Hike

This trail is for the adventurous hiker only. It goes through the most remote and rugged part of Guadalupe Mountains National Park. You can get your backcountry camping permit at the Dog Canyon Ranger Station, just north of the trailhead.

This trip could be done in one very long day of strenuous walking, but this would be too much for most hikers. Instead, take it more slowly and enjoy it by making this an overnighter. For an even more relaxed pace, spend three nights out, each at a different backcountry campsite. To save the steepest and most rugged parts of the loop for the end of the trip, take the clockwise route as described here.

Shortly after leaving Dog Canyon trailhead, you'll see the Bush Mountain Trail coming in from the right (west). You'll be dragging down this trail on your way out.

Turn left (south) on the Tejas Trail, which follows a burnt, but still beautiful, riparian zone along Dog Canyon for about 1.5 miles to Dog Canyon Springs. Here the trail takes a sharp right and starts to switchback up toward Lost Peak. After another 1.5 miles you go by Lost Peak on your right. This is a good spot to drop your pack and scramble up to the top for a great view and a needed rest.

In another mile or so, you hit the junction with the McKittrick Canyon Trail coming in from the left (east). Take a right, staying on the Tejas Trail.

If you are staying out three nights, you'll want to stop at the Mescalero camp, another 0.8 mile down the trail on your left. Mescalero camp has eight tent sites, with number 1 the best room in the inn.

If you're staying only one night, however, you'll want to blow by Mescalero camp and head for Blue Ridge camp. You'll see the junction with the Blue Ridge Trail about 0.7 mile past Mescalero camp. Turn right (west) and start climbing up to the Marcus Trail. In 0.5 mile you'll see the Blue Ridge heading off to the right (north). Keep going west (and climbing) to the Blue Ridge Trail for another 1.2 miles, until you see the Blue Ridge camp on your right. The first 0.5 mile past the junction with the Marcus Trail is a serious climb—short but steep on a rocky trail with a series of tight switchbacks.

Looking south toward Bush Mountain, the wildest and roughest part of Guadalupe Mountains National Park.

If you're out for only one night, this is your best campsite. The Blue Ridge camp is shaded by stately Douglas fir and ponderosa pine, plus a few large oak trees. It has five tent sites.

After a pleasant night on the Blue Ridge, the tough hiking begins. For another scenic 0.5 mile, you continue to straddle the Blue Ridge. Then take a right at the junction with the Bush Mountain Trail.

Shortly after this junction you enter the burn of the 1994 Marcus Fire, and the trail gets rough and rocky and, at times, hard to find. A few brown National Park Service trail markers mark the way. This trail traditionally received minimal use, so it was not as well defined as most other trails in the park.

Try to look at the fire as a natural phenomenon instead of a destructive force. Also, look at it as a short-term distraction. Fire is an essential part of nature, and in many cases it's essential to the long-term health of the area's fauna and flora.

As you head down toward West Dog Canyon, you'll be happy with your decision to take the clockwise route. The trail drops steeply after leaving the Blue Ridge, and you wouldn't want to climb this hill with a big pack.

If you want to be alone, this is the place. Very few hikers use this trail compared to others in the park.

The Blue Ridge Trail.

After about 1.5 miles, the trail levels off and goes through open, gently rolling country all the way to West Dog Canyon. Before this area became a national park, it was ranchland, and even today you can see signs of the past—old fences, tanks, and the remains of ranch buildings.

Just before you reach the Marcus Trail coming down West Dog Canyon, watch for the Marcus camp off to your left. If you're out for three nights, this is your third campsite.

You'll find the junction with the Marcus Trail right in the bottom of West Dog Canyon. Take a good break here, because the next 1.5 miles up to Manzanita Ridge will be the toughest climb of the entire trip. Besides being steep, this section of trail is rough and rocky. On top, finally, you'll find a hitching rail for horses and a great view. Even better is the news that it's a gradual downhill the last 2 miles back to the Dog Canyon trailhead.

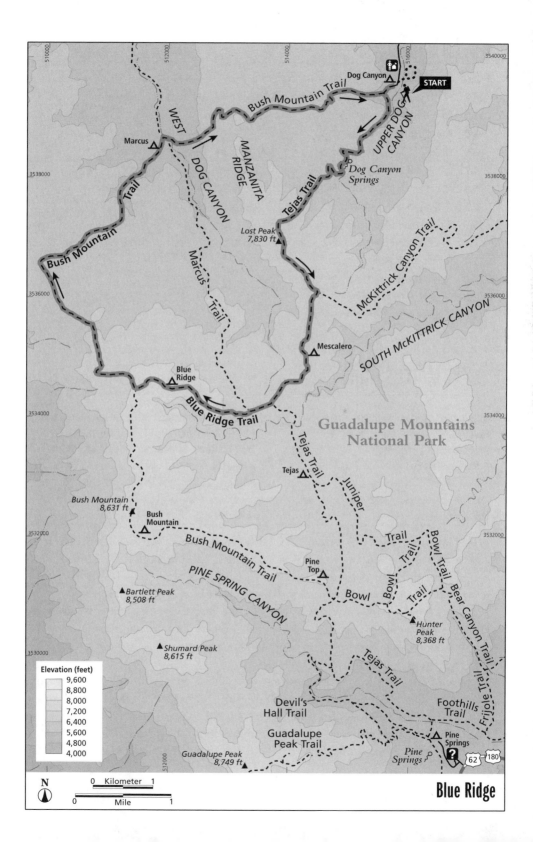

Blue Ridge

Miles and Directions

0.0 Start at the Dog Canyon campground.

0.1 At the junction with Bush Mountain Trail, turn left onto the Tejas Trail.

1.5 Pass Dog Canyon Springs.

3.0 Pass Lost Peak on the right.

3.9 At the junction with McKittrick Canyon Trail, turn right, staying on the Tejas Trail.

4.7 Reach the Mescalero camp.

5.4 At the junction with Blue Ridge Trail, turn right, climbing up to the Marcus Trail.

5.7 At the junction with Marcus Trail, turn left, staying on the Blue Ridge Trail.

6.9 Arrive at the Blue Ridge camp.

7.4 At the junction with Bush Mountain Trail, turn right.

11.1 Reach the Marcus camp.

11.3 Reach the junction with Marcus Trail.

12.8 Crest Manzanita Ridge.

14.8 Return to Dog Canyon trailhead.

34 Marcus Trail

Highlights: Serious overnight trip.
Start: Dog Canyon campground.
Distance: 13.1-mile loop.
Difficulty: Difficult.

Maps: Trails Illustrated: Guadalupe Mountains; USGS: Guadalupe Peak; park brochure.
Trail contact: Guadalupe Mountains National Park, H.C. 60, Box 400, Salt Flat, TX 79847-9400; (915) 828-3251; www.nps.gov/gamo.

The Hike

If you hike this loop counterclockwise (as described here), you can avoid the precipitous 1.5-mile climb up from West Dog Canyon to Manzanita Ridge. If you stay overnight at the Mescalero camp, this makes the first day a rough 8.4-mile hike, but it saves you the pain of climbing this steep pitch with an overnight pack.

Whichever way you hike it, however, it's still a long 13.1 miles with a 1,500-foot elevation gain. You can make it a long day hike or take your time and stay overnight at Mescalero camp. You can get your backcountry permit at the Dog Canyon Ranger Station, just north of the trailhead.

Shortly after you leave the Dog Canyon trailhead on the Tejas Trail, you reach the junction with the Bush Mountain Trail. Turn right (west) on the Bush Mountain Trail. You'll be coming down the Tejas Trail at the end of your hike.

In about 2 miles, a moderately steep climb through the burn of the 1994 Marcus Fire, you top out on Manzanita Ridge. Up to this point the trail is in great

Upper end of West Dog Canyon from the Marcus Trail.

shape, but it turns steep and rocky as you crest the divide and head down to West Dog Canyon. This can be difficult footing with a big pack, but you'll be overjoyed you aren't climbing up this hill.

At the bottom of West Dog Canyon, you'll see the junction with the Marcus Trail. Take a left (south) and head for the heart of the Guadalupe Mountains. Be careful you take the Marcus Trail and not the Bush Mountain Trail, which continues on in a southerly direction. The Marcus Trail is a reclaimed jeep road, which means the grade is not that steep, but it's steadily uphill all the way to the Blue Ridge Trail.

Parts of the first half of the trail to Blue Ridge can be difficult to find, so be alert for cairns, especially where the trail leaves the valley floor and switchbacks up to the ridge on the west side of West Dog Canyon. After a mile or so on the ridge, the trail enters the high-altitude forest of the Guadalupes and turns into a delightful path carpeted with pine needles and oak leaves. It stays like this until you hit the Blue Ridge Trail.

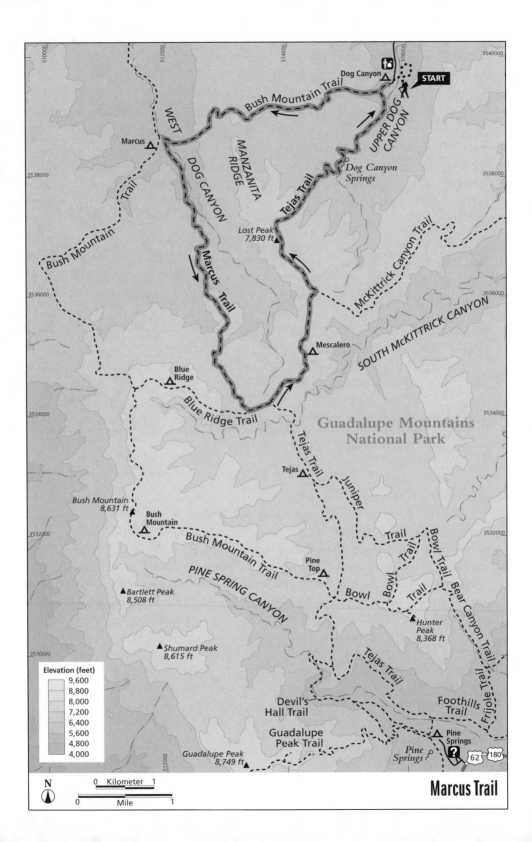

Dog Canyon △

👤 START

Bush Mountain Trail

←

→

WEST

Marcus △

DOG CANYON

MANZANITA RIDGE

UPPER DOG CANYON

○ Dog Canyon Springs

Tejas Trail

Lost Peak 7,830 ft ▲

←

McKittrick Canyon Trail

Marcus Trail

↓

SOUTH McKITTRICK CANYON

Mescalero △

Blue Ridge △

Blue Ridge Trail

↑

Guadalupe Mountains National Park

Tejas Trail

Tejas △

Juniper

Bush Mountain 8,631 ft ▲

Bush Mountain △

Bush Mountain Trail

PINE SPRING CANYON

Pine Top △

Trail

Bowl Trail

Bowl

Bowl Trail

Bear Canyon Trail

Frijole Trail

Bowl Trail

▲ Bartlett Peak 8,508 ft

▲ Hunter Peak 8,368 ft

▲ Shumard Peak 8,615 ft

Tejas Trail

Devil's Hall Trail

Foothills Trail

Guadalupe Peak Trail

Pine Springs △

Pine Springs ○

❓

62 180

▲ Guadalupe Peak 8,749 ft

Elevation (feet)
9,600
8,800
8,000
7,200
6,400
5,600
4,800
4,000

N

0   Kilometer   1

0   Mile   1

Marcus Trail

At the Blue Ridge junction, turn left (east) and head down 0.5 mile to the Tejas Trail junction. Take a left (north) here and go another 0.7 mile to the Mescalero camp on your right. Mescalero camp has eight tent sites, with number 1 offering the best view and most privacy.

After an enjoyable night at the Mescalero camp, get up early to take advantage of the cool morning air as you head north back to the trailhead. Hiking early and quietly increases your chances of seeing elk, deer, turkey, and other wildlife common in this area. On your right on your way to the junction with McKittrick Canyon Trail are the spectacular upper reaches of South McKittrick Canyon, preserved as a Research Natural Area by the National Park Service, with no entry allowed. This one spot in the Guadalupes will remain totally untrampled by *Homo sapiens*.

At the junction with the McKittrick Canyon Trail, take a left and continue through the rich forest toward Lost Peak. Shortly beyond Lost Peak the forest opens up and you switchback down a ridge into the depths of Dog Canyon, coming out at Dog Canyon Springs. From that point on you follow the easy grade of the canyon bottom all the way to the trailhead.

Miles and Directions

0.0   Start at Dog Canyon campground on the Tejas Trail.

0.1   At the junction with Bush Mountain Trail, turn right.

2.5   Crest the divide between Dog Canyon and West Dog Canyon.

3.5   In West Dog Canyon at the junction with Marcus Trail, turn left.

7.4   At the junction with Blue Ridge Trail, turn left.

7.7   At the junction with Tejas Trail, turn left.

8.4   Reach the Mescalero camp.

9.2   At the junction with McKittrick Canyon Trail, turn left.

10.0 Pass Lost Peak.

13.1 Return to Dog Canyon trailhead.

35 Tejas Trail

Highlights: A fantastic trip through the entire mountain range, but only possible with a lengthy vehicle shuttle.
Start: Dog Canyon campground.
Distance: 11.4-mile shuttle.
Difficulty: Difficult day trip or moderate overnighter.

Maps: Trails Illustrated: Guadalupe Mountains; USGS: Guadalupe Peak and PX Flat; park brochure.
Trail contact: Guadalupe Mountains National Park, H.C. 60, Box 400, Salt Flat, TX 79847-9400; (915) 828-3251; www.nps.gov/gamo.

The Hike

If you want to walk all the way through the Guadalupe Mountains, this is the shortest and easiest route with the least possible elevation gain, mainly because the Dog Canyon trailhead is at a fairly high elevation (6,290 feet).

Regrettably, however, it involves a difficult shuttle. The best way to take this trip would be to make a deal with another party to meet at the Tejas camp and trade keys so you can drive each other's vehicle to a rendezvous point. If this option isn't available, however, you'll simply have to beg or buy a ride to Dog Canyon, leaving your vehicle at Pine Springs. It will be worth the money or humility. This is a great trip. You can make this a long day hike, but you'll probably enjoy it more as an overnighter.

After getting your backcountry permit from the ranger station at Dog Canyon or the Pine Springs Visitor Center, try to start early. As you quietly walk along the riparian zone of Dog Canyon, you're likely to see wild turkey, mule deer, and other wildlife.

You leave the gradual grade of the canyon bottom at Dog Canyon Springs as the trail takes a sharp right turn and starts switchbacking up an open ridge leading to Lost Peak. Just before Lost Peak the trail enters the forest and stays there until you reach the edge of the escarpment above Pine Springs Canyon. This stretch may be the best trail in the Guadalupes. It's fairly level for 5 miles, well maintained, and not rocky like some trails in the park.

About a mile past Lost Peak, you hit the junction with the McKittrick Canyon Trail. Turn right and keep going south on the Tejas Trail.

In 0.8 mile you go by the Mescalero camp on your left. You can stay here, but the Tejas camp is more centrally located 1.5 miles down the trail. When you reach the junction with the Blue Ridge Trail, 0.7 mile past the Mescalero camp, take a left and keep heading south on the Tejas Trail for another 0.8 mile to the Tejas camp.

The Tejas camp has four tent sites, with number 1 providing the best view. In the camp you'll find an old water tank, a reminder of early ranching activities in the area.

The relict, high-altitude forest of the Guadalupe Mountains.

Shortly after you leave the Tejas camp, you hit the junction with the Juniper Trail. (Although this trail description covers the Tejas Trail all the way to Pine Springs, there is an alternative route. At this point you could lengthen your trip by 1 mile and follow the Juniper Trail down to Bear Canyon Trail and back to the Pine Springs trailhead via the Frijole and Foothill Trails.) To stay on the Tejas Trail, take a right at this junction, and enjoy your last 1.5 miles of forest-lined trail until you hit the junction with the Bowl Trail at the edge of the escarpment overlooking the Pine Springs area.

At this point you might want to drop your pack and take a short side-trip to "the best view in Texas" from the top of Hunter Peak. From the junction it's a 2-mile round-trip to Hunter Peak and back—and well worth it. (On the alternative route, the side-trip to Hunter Peak is only 1 mile total, which cancels out the extra mileage and makes the two routes almost exactly the same distance.)

After the side-trip and a good rest, head down the escarpment on a well-constructed trail, leaving the relict forest of the Guadalupes behind. You trade the quiet serenity of the forest for the awesome vistas of the upper stretches of this trail.

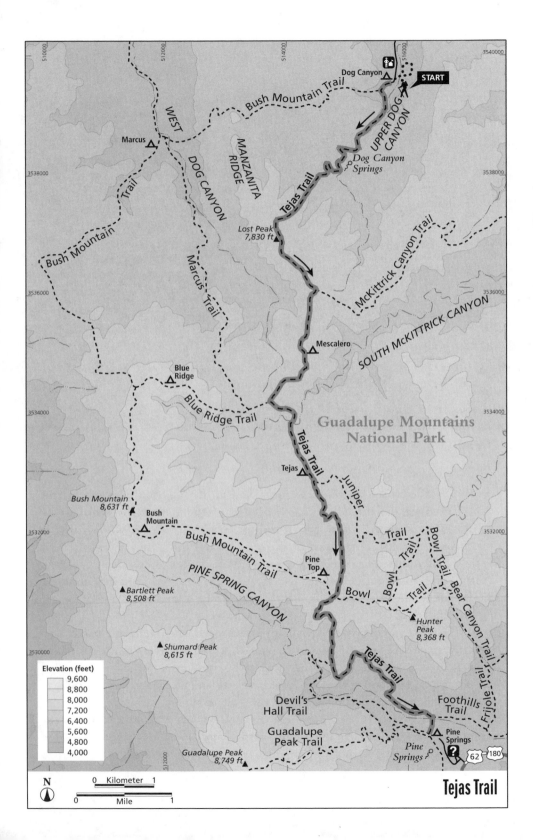

You get great views of Pine Springs Canyon, plus Guadalupe, Shumard, and Bartlett peaks, which highlight the ridge on the other side of the canyon. You also get a great chance to study the sharp contrast between the vegetative community of the high plateau and the desert below.

At the bottom of the canyon, you hit the junction with the Frijole Trail. Take a right, staying on the Tejas Trail across the gigantic dry wash of Pine Springs Canyon, where you hit another junction. Turn left and you are at Pine Springs trailhead in another 100 feet.

Miles and Directions

0.0 Start at the Dog Canyon campground on the Tejas Trail.

0.1 At the junction with Bush Mountain Trail, turn left.

1.5 Pass Dog Canyon Springs.

3.0 Pass Lost Peak on the right.

3.9 At the junction with McKittrick Canyon Trail, turn right.

4.7 Reach the Mescalero camp.

5.4 At the junction with Blue Ridge Trail, turn left.

6.2 Reach the Tejas camp.

6.5 At the junction with Juniper Trail, turn right. **Option:** Take a left to follow the Juniper Trail down to Bear Canyon Trail and back to the Pine Springs trailhead via the Frijole and Foothill Trails.

7.7 At the junction with Bowl and Bush Mountain Trails, go straight. **Side-trip:** Turn left onto Bowl Trail and then right on the spur trail to Hunter Peak for a great view. It's a 2-mile round-trip from the junction to Hunter Peak and back.

11.3 At the junction with Frijole Trail, turn right.

11.4 Turn left at the next junction and arrive at Pine Springs trailhead.

36 Dog Canyon to McKittrick Canyon

Highlights: A fantastic trip through the entire mountain range, but only possible with a lengthy vehicle shuttle.
Start: Dog Canyon campground.
Distance: 14.9-mile shuttle.
Difficulty: Difficult day trip or moderate overnighter.

Maps: Trails Illustrated: Guadalupe Mountains; USGS: Guadalupe Peak and PX Flat; park brochure.
Trail contact: Guadalupe Mountains National Park, H.C. 60, Box 400, Salt Flat, TX 79847-9400; (915) 828–3251; www.nps.gov/gamo.

The Hike

This is a great way to get the ultimate view of McKittrick Canyon because you don't have to climb up "the Big Sweat," the steep climb out of McKittrick Canyon. However, it involves a problematic shuttle.

The first order of business is to arrange that shuttle. You have to get yourself to Dog Canyon and arrange for a pickup or a vehicle to be left at McKittrick Canyon Visitor Center. You can also do a "trade keys" trip with friends or relatives and camp together at McKittrick Ridge camp, but this plan may result in a drawn-out debate over who gets to start at Dog Canyon. The loser has to face the nearly 2,600-foot climb out of McKittrick Canyon. You can get your backcountry camping permit at either Dog Canyon Ranger Station (just north of the trailhead) or the Pine Springs Visitor Center.

Immediately after leaving the Dog Canyon trailhead on the Tejas Trail, you hit the junction with the Bush Mountain Trail. You take a left and follow narrowing Dog Canyon until the trail turns sharply to the right at Dog Canyon Springs and starts climbing out of the canyon. In another 1.5 miles of steady climbing, you might be ready for a break. If so, drop your pack and hike a short distance to the top of Lost Peak for a good rest and a great view. Then continue on for another mile to the junction with the McKittrick Canyon Trail.

Turn left (east) here and follow the fairly level trail along McKittrick Ridge. Virtually all the way to McKittrick Ridge camp, you have good views of the entire Guadalupe high country, especially the upper reaches of South McKittrick Canyon.

You could do this trail in one long day, but most hikers prefer to stay overnight at McKittrick Ridge camp, which is on your left 3.5 miles after you leave the Tejas Trail. Even though the camp is nestled in a elegant grove of trees, the view from the camp is inferior to the view from the trail. The camp has eight tent sites, with number 1 and number 8 providing the most privacy.

After leaving camp the next morning, you pass through a forest that blocks much of the view for a mile or so. Then you break out of the trees and before you is the hidden jewel of the Guadalupes, McKittrick Canyon. From up here you can see that

Looking down into Dog Canyon from the Tejas Trail.

the north-facing slopes of the canyon support more riparian species than the drier south-facing slopes.

The view stays with you like a panoramic movie screen for the next 2 miles as you descend "the Big Sweat." You will be elated that you didn't do the trip in reverse.

After 4.1 miles you see a spur trail to the right leading to the Grotto. You'll want to drop your pack here and hike the 0.1 mile to the Grotto (which is like a cave caught above ground) and Hunter Line Cabin. A 5,632-acre gift by the Pratt family and a 70,000-acre purchase from the Hunter family combined to form the bulk of what is now Guadalupe Mountains National Park.

At the Grotto you find a unique feature of the arid Guadalupes—out of the canyon flows a large stream that's large enough to support a population of rainbow trout. The stream stays on your right for another 1.1 miles, until you reach another short spur trail to your left going to Pratt Lodge. Here you can take a long breather and picnic on the stone tables found near the lodge. After leaving the stately Pratt Lodge, it's an easy 2.3 miles to the McKittrick Canyon Visitor Center. Over these last miles the stream magically disappears and reappears several times.

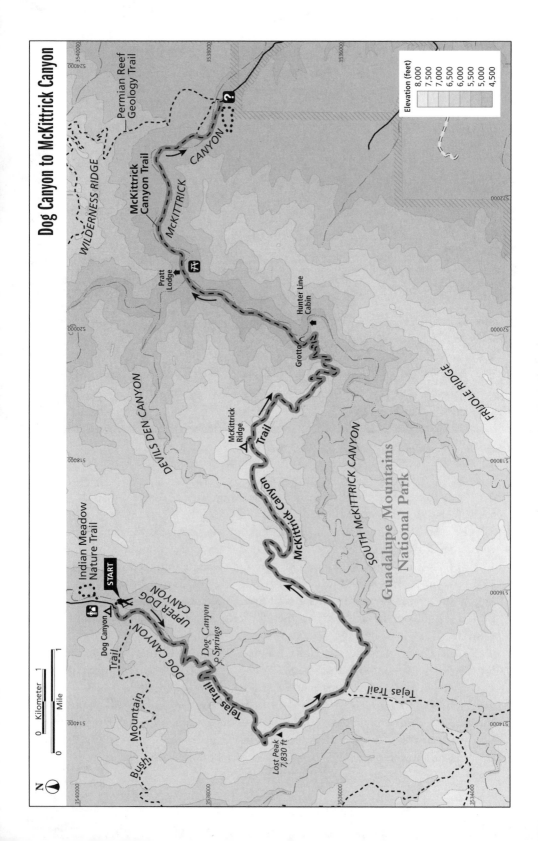

Dog Canyon to McKittrick Canyon

N

0 Kilometer 1

0 Mile 1

Bush Mountain

Dog Canyon Trail

DOG CANYON

Dog Canyon

Indian Meadow Nature Trail

START

UPPER DOG CANYON

Dog Canyon Springs

Tejas Trail

Lost Peak 7,830 ft

Tejas Trail

McKittrick Canyon Trail

DEVILS DEN CANYON

McKittrick Ridge

McKittrick Ridge Trail

SOUTH McKITTRICK CANYON

Guadalupe Mountains National Park

FRIJOLE RIDGE

Grotto

Hunter Line Cabin

Pratt Lodge

WILDERNESS RIDGE

Permian Reef Geology Trail

McKITTRICK CANYON

McKittrick Canyon Trail

?

Elevation (feet)

8,000
7,500
7,000
6,500
6,000
5,500
5,000
4,500

Make sure you plan your trip to leave enough time to drive the 4.5 miles from the visitor center to U.S. Highway 62/180. The National Park Service locks the gate at 6:00 P.M. when daylight savings time is in effect and 4:30 P.M. during standard time.

Miles and Directions

0.0 Start at the Dog Canyon campground on the Tejas Trail.

0.1 At the junction with Bush Mountain Trail, turn left.

3.0 Pass Lost Peak on the right. **Side-trip:** Hike a short distance to the top of Lost Peak. Return to the main trail.

3.9 At the junction with the McKittrick Canyon Trail, turn left.

7.4 Reach the McKittrick Ridge camp. Continue along the McKittrick Canyon Trail.

11.5 Follow a spur trail on the right to the Grotto and Hunter Line Cabin. Return to the main trail.

12.6 Arrive at Pratt Lodge.

14.9 Finish at McKittrick Canyon trailhead.

Afterword: The Value of Guidebooks

Some people don't like hiking guidebooks. They believe guidebooks bring more people into the wilderness; more people cause more environmental damage; and the wildness we all seek gradually evaporates. I used to believe that too. Here's why I changed my mind.

When I wrote and published my first guidebook in 1979, some of my hiking buddies disapproved, and I spent a lot of time up in the mountains thinking about the value of guidebooks. Since then I've published more than a hundred hiking guides (and have written eleven myself), and I'm proud of it. I also hope these books have significantly increased wilderness use.

A few experienced hikers have lofty attitudes toward the inexperienced masses. They think anybody can buy a topographic map and compass and find his or her way through the wilderness. But the fact is most people want a guide. Sometimes inexperienced hikers prefer a live person to show them the way and help them build confidence, but most of the time they can get by with a trail guide like this one.

All guidebooks published by Falcon (and most published by other publishers) encourage wilderness users to respect the wilderness and support the protection of wild country. Sometimes this message is direct editorializing, but more often it's subliminal. By helping people enjoy wilderness, the guidebook publisher sets up a format where the message naturally creeps into the soul. It's a rare person who leaves the wilderness without a firmly planted passion for wild country—and an interest in voting for more of it.

In classes on backpacking that I've taught for the Yellowstone Institute, I've taken hundreds of people into the wilderness. Many of them had a backpack on for the first time. When we started our hike, some of them weren't convinced we needed more wilderness, but they all were convinced that we did when they arrived back at the trailhead. Many, many times I've seen it happen without saying a single word about wilderness preservation efforts.

It doesn't take preaching. Instead, we just need to get people out into the wilderness, where the essence of wildness sort of sneaks up on them and takes root, and before you know it the ranks of those who support wilderness has grown. I'd go as far to say that in today's political world, it's difficult to get people to support more wilderness if they haven't experienced it for themselves. I recently returned from a long backpacking trip in the Arctic National Wildlife Refuge in Alaska, which is on the menu of the oil industry. I have no doubt that if people could experience what I did on that trip, they would fervently oppose drilling in the refuge.

But what about overcrowding? Yes, it is a problem in many places and probably will be in many wilderness areas. But the answer to overcrowded, overused wilderness is not limiting use of wilderness and restrictive regulations. The answer is more wilderness. And even if we must endure more restrictions, so be it. At least we—and our children and grandchildren—will always have a wild place to enjoy, even if we can't go there every weekend. The landscape can recover from overcrowding, but if we build roads and houses there, it's gone forever.

That's why we need guidebooks, and that's why I changed my mind. I actually believe guidebooks have done as much to build support for wilderness as pro-wilderness organizations have ever done through political and public relations efforts.

And if that isn't enough, here's another reason. All FalconGuides (and most guidebooks from other publishers) contain sections on zero-impact ethics. Guide-books provide the ideal medium for communicating such vital information.

In thirty-five years of hiking, I've seen dramatic changes in how hikers care for wilderness. I've seen it go from appalling to exceptional. Through the years I've car-ried tons of foil and litter out of the wilderness, and I've probably destroyed more fire rings than almost anybody on earth. But nowadays I can enjoy a weeklong trip without finding a gum wrapper or tissue. Today almost everybody walks softly in the wilderness. And I believe the information contained in guidebooks has been partly responsible for this positive change.

Having said all that, I hope many thousands of people use this book to enjoy a fun-filled hiking vacation—and then, of course, vote for wilderness protection and encourage others to do the same.

—*Bill Schneider*

Vacation Planner

Carlsbad Caverns National Park

Trails for People with Mobility Impairments

    Hike 1: Chihuahuan Desert Nature Trail

Easy Day Hikes

    Hike 2: Guano Road Trail

    Hike 3: Juniper Ridge

Moderate Day Trips

    Hike 4: Rattlesnake Canyon

Difficult Day Trips

    Hike 5: Guadalupe Ridge

    Hike 6: Slaughter Canyon

    Hike 7: Yucca Canyon

Overnight Trips

    Hike 4: Rattlesnake Canyon

    Hike 5: Guadalupe Ridge

    Hike 6: Slaughter Canyon

    Hike 7: Yucca Canyon

Guadalupe Mountains National Park

Trails for People with Mobility Impairments

    Hike 16: The Pinery

    Hike 23: Smith Spring (to Manzanita Spring only)

Easy Day Hikes

    Hike 23: Smith Spring

    Hike 27: McKittrick Canyon Nature Trail

    Hike 28: McKittrick Canyon (to Pratt Lodge)

    Hike 31: Indian Meadow Nature Trail

Moderate Day Trips

    Hike 17: Salt Basin Overlook

    Hike 20: Devil's Hall

    Hike 24: Foothills

    Hike 28: McKittrick Canyon (to the Grotto)

    Hike 32: Lost Peak

Difficult Day Trips

Hike 18: El Capitan

Hike 19: Guadalupe Peak

Hike 21: Hunter Peak

Hike 22: The Bowl

Hike 28: McKittrick Canyon (to the Notch)

Hike 30: Permian Reef

Hike 35: Tejas Trail

Overnight Trips

Hike 19: Guadalupe Peak

Hike 21: Hunter Peak

Hike 22: The Bowl

Hike 25: Bush Mountain

Hike 26: Pine Springs to McKittrick Canyon

Hike 29: McKittrick Ridge

Hike 30: Permian Reef

Hike 33: Blue Ridge

Hike 34: Marcus Trail

Hike 35: Tejas Trail

Hike 36: Dog Canyon to McKittrick Canyon

Author's Recommendations

Carlsbad Caverns National Park

For Parents Who Want a Really Easy Day Hike
Hike 1: Chihuahuan Desert Nature Trail

For People Who Want an Easy—But Not Too Easy—Day Hike
Hike 2: Guano Road Trail
Hike 3: Juniper Ridge

For People Who Can't Decide between a Long Hike or a Short Hike, So Obviously Need a Moderately Difficult Hike
Hike 4: Rattlesnake Canyon

For People Who Want a Long, Hard Day Hike So at the End of the Day They Can Eat Anything They Want for Dinner and Not Feel Guilty
Hike 5: Guadalupe Ridge
Hike 6: Slaughter Canyon
Hike 7: Yucca Canyon

For That First Night in the Wilderness
Hike 4: Rattlesnake Canyon

For Photographers
Hike 4: Rattlesnake Canyon
Hike 5: Guadalupe Ridge
Hike 7: Yucca Canyon

For People Who Want a Multiday Backcountry Adventure
Hike 5: Guadalupe Ridge
Hike 6: Slaughter Canyon (loop route)

For Trail Runners and Power Hikers
Hike 2: Guano Road Trail
Hike 5: Guadalupe Ridge

Guadalupe Mountains National Park

For Parents Who Want a Really Easy Day Hike
Hike 16: The Pinery
Hike 27: McKittrick Canyon Nature Trail
Hike 31: Indian Meadow Nature Trail

For People Who Want an Easy—But Not Too Easy—Day Hike

Hike 23: Smith Spring
Hike 28: McKittrick Canyon (to Pratt Lodge)

For People Who Can't Decide between a Long Hike or a Short Hike, So Obviously Need a Moderately Difficult Hike

Hike 17: Salt Basin Overlook
Hike 20: Devil's Hall
Hike 24: Foothills
Hike 32: Lost Peak

For People Who Want a Long, Hard Day Hike So at the End of the Day They Can Eat Anything They Want for Dinner and Not Feel Guilty

Hike 17: Salt Basin Overlook
Hike 18: El Capitan (one way)
Hike 19: Guadalupe Peak
Hike 21: Hunter Peak
Hike 28: McKittrick Canyon (to the Notch)
Hike 30: Permian Reef
Hike 35: Tejas Trail

For That First Night in the Wilderness

Hike 21: Hunter Peak
Hike 35: Tejas Trail

For Photographers

Hike 17: Salt Basin Overlook
Hike 18: El Capitan
Hike 19: Guadalupe Peak
Hike 21: Hunter Peak
Hike 28: McKittrick Canyon (to the Notch)
Hike 30: Permian Reef

For People Who Want a Multiday Backcountry Adventure

Hike 18: El Capitan (out and back)
Hike 25: Bush Mountain
Hike 26: Pine Springs to McKittrick Canyon
Hike 35: Tejas Trail
Hike 36: Dog Canyon to McKittrick Canyon

For People Who Want to See the Wildest Part of the Guadalupe Mountains

Hike 25: Bush Mountain
Hike 33: Blue Ridge
Hike 34: Marcus Trail

For Trail Runners and Power Hikers

Hike 17: Salt Basin Overlook

Hike 18: El Capitan

Hike 19: Guadalupe Peak

Hike 26: Pine Springs to McKittrick Canyon

Hike 28: McKittrick Canyon (to the Grotto)

Hike 30: Permian Reef

Hike 35: Tejas Trail

Hike 36: Dog Canyon to McKittrick Canyon

For People Who Want to Walk All the Way through the Guadalupe Mountains

Hike 26: Pine Springs to McKittrick Canyon

Hike 35: Tejas Trail

About the Author

Bill Schneider has spent thirty-five years hiking trails all across America. During college in the mid-1960s, he worked on a trail crew in Glacier National Park and became a hiking addict. He spent the 1970s publishing the *Montana Outdoors* magazine for the Montana Department of Fish, Wildlife & Parks while covering as many miles of trails as possible on weekends and holidays. In 1979 Bill and his partner, Mike Sample, founded Falcon Publishing. Since then he has written twenty books and many magazine articles on wildlife, outdoor recreation, and environmental issues. Bill has also taught classes on bicycling, backpacking, zero-impact camping, and hiking in bear country for the Yellowstone Institute, a nonprofit educational organization in Yellowstone National Park.

In 2000 Bill retired from his position as president of Falcon Publishing (now part of The Globe Pequot Press) after it had grown into the premier publisher of outdoor recreation guidebooks, with more than 700 titles in print. He now lives in Helena, Montana, with his wife, Marnie, and works as a publishing consultant and freelance writer.

The author on top of Guadalupe Peak.

Books by Bill Schneider

Learn more about Bill Schneider's books at www.billschneider.net.

Where the Grizzly Walks, 1977

Hiking Montana, 1979, last revised 2004

The Dakota Image, 1980

The Yellowstone River, 1985

Best Hikes on the Continental Divide, 1988

The Flight of the Nez Perce, 1988

The Tree Giants, 1988

Hiking the Beartooths, 1995

Bear Aware, A Quick Reference Bear Country Survival Guide, 1996, last revised 2004

Hiking Carlsbad Caverns and Guadalupe Mountains National Parks, 1996, last revised 2005

Best Easy Day Hikes Yellowstone, 1997, last revised 2003

Exploring Canyonlands and Arches National Parks, 1997, last revised 2005

Hiking Yellowstone National Park, 1997, last revised 2003

Backpacking Tips, co-author, 1998

Best Easy Day Hikes Beartooths, 1998

Best Easy Day Hikes Grand Teton, 1999, last revised 2005

Hiking Grand Teton National Park, 1999, last revised 2005

Best Backpacking Vacations Northern Rockies, 2002

Hiking the Absaroka-Beartooth Wilderness, 2003

Where the Grizzly Walks, 2003

WHAT'S SO SPECIAL ABOUT UNSPOILED, NATURAL PLACES?

Beauty Solitude Wildness Freedom Quiet Adventure
Serenity Inspiration Wonder Excitement
Relaxation Challenge

There's a lot to love about our treasured public lands, and the reasons are different for each of us. Whatever your reasons are, the national **Leave No Trace** education program will help you discover special outdoor places, enjoy them, and preserve them—today and for those who follow. By practicing and passing along these simple principles, you can help protect the special places you love from being loved to death.

THE PRINCIPLES OF **LEAVE NO TRACE**

- Plan ahead and prepare
- Travel and camp on durable surfaces
- Dispose of waste properly
- Leave what you find
- Minimize campfire impacts
- Respect wildlife
- Be considerate of other visitors

LEAVE NO TRACE
OUTDOOR ETHICS

Leave No Trace is a national nonprofit organization dedicated to teaching responsible outdoor recreation skills and ethics to everyone who enjoys spending time outdoors.

To learn more or to become a member, please visit us at www.LNT.org or call (800) 332-4100.

Leave No Trace, P.O. Box 997, Boulder, CO 80306

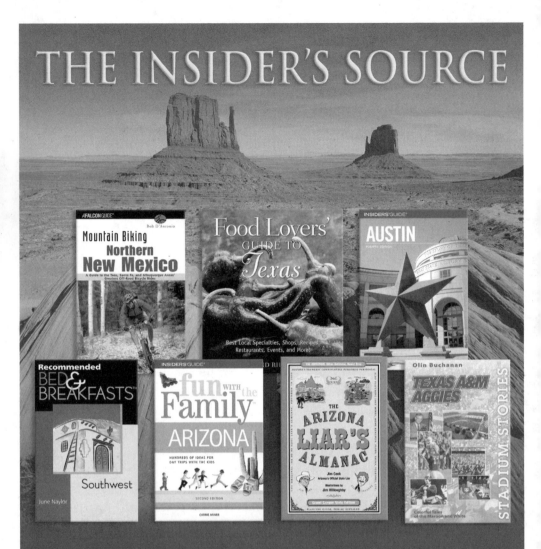